JUNE OSBORNE

Hampton Court PALACE

Hampton Court Palace welcomes the return to print of Mrs Osborne's book.

LONDON: HMSO

ILLUSTRATIONS

HMSO publications are available from:

HMSO Publications Centre
(Mail and telephone orders only)
PO Box 276, London, SW8 5DT
Telephone orders 01-873 9090
General enquiries 01-873 0011
(queuing system in operation for both numbers)

HMSO Bookshops
49 High Holborn, London, WC1V 6HB   01-873 0011 (Counter service only)
258 Broad Street, Birmingham, B1 2HE   021-643 3740
Southey House, 33 Wine Street, Bristol, BS1 2BQ   (0272) 264306
9-21 Princess Street, Manchester, M60 8AS   061-834 7201
80 Chichester Street, Belfast, BT1 4JY   (0232) 238451
71 Lothian Road, Edinburgh, EH3 9AZ   031-228 4181

HMSO's Accredited Agents
(see Yellow Pages)

and through good booksellers

From 6 May 1990 the London telephone numbers
above carry the prefix '071' instead of '01'.

© June Osborne 1984
First published Kaye and Ward 1984
This impression published by HMSO 1990

ISBN 0 11 290484 X

Printed in the United Kingdom for HMSO
Dd 291281 C40 4/90 63215

Contents

ACKNOWLEDGEMENTS

It is impossible to write a book on Hampton Court Palace without reference to the books, articles and letters of that assiduous and painstaking historian Ernest Law and, though he has been dead for more than half a century now, my first debt is to him.

There was a need, however, for something more succinct and accessible than Law's three-volume work (long since out of print). Also the history had to be brought up to date, revised in the light of more recent research into past centuries, and the story completed up to the present day. In my attempt to fulfil this need I owe much to the help of all my fellow guide-lecturers at Hampton Court Palace, especially Marie Everett for her generous assistance in many different aspects of putting the book together, Gerald Heath for allowing me the benefit of his meticulous research, and also Mary Connatty. I am very grateful too, to Rita Larner, the Photographic Librarian of the Department of the Environment, for all her generous help and advice, and to Joe Cowell, Superintendent of the Royal Collection at Hampton Court, for his careful perusal of my writing concering the paintings, and for lending me photographs and newscuttings. Ian Gray, Superintendent of the Palace, has helped me generally, and kindly made Ernest Law's scrapbooks available for my perusal, Jenny Band of the Textile Conservation Studios has provided a most useful report on the work being done on the furniture; meanwhile in all my dealings with the Lord Chamberlain's Office (in particular Marcus Bishop) and the Department of the Environment (in particular Peter Curnow, Brian Bayliss and John Thorneycroft), I have met with nothing but courtesy and helpfulness.

I must also acknowledge the assistance given me by the staff of Twickenham Reference Library, the Public Record Office, and the Library of the Royal Institute of British Architects. Peter Miall, Historic Buildings Representative of the National Trust, and Richard Wakeford, Administrator at Knole House, have also helped me.

I am most indebted to all my children, especially to my elder daughter Elizabeth for assisting me with typing and editing the manuscript, as well as photography, to my twins Patrick and Jane for helping me prepare the text and to my elder son Ian for friendly advice. In short, they have been wonderfully co-operative in all sorts of ways while the book was in writing, and I give them my thanks. I am grateful too, to Sir Huw Wheldon for kindly agreeing to write a foreword to this book, and to my friend Nigel Foxell for his continuing encouragement.

JUNE OSBORNE
November 1983

FOREWORD

There is little doubt that the glories of Hampton Court Palace owe more to William of Orange, and to his tall, shy and elegant wife Queen Mary II, than is generally assumed. Cardinal Wolsey and Henry VIII are names that spring to mind. But it was William and Mary who invited Sir Christopher Wren to add a new and contemporary magnificence to the historical splendours of the existing buildings. It was clearly imperative that the new King and Queen should live in a Palace which matched the opulent surroundings in which King Louis XIV of France had his being. The original Tudor Palace, for all its majesty, would need extension. Besides which, it was probably somewhat run down, having been treated with a fair amount of contempt during the Protectorate.

The new monarchs had opted immediately for Hampton Court as their main residence. William suffered from asthma. He hated the dust and smoke of Westminster and St James's and needed clean air; and equally it certainly suited the gentle and modest disposition of Queen Mary to spend her days in the tranquillity of the Thames Valley, rather than in the bustle of London itself.

Sir Christopher Wren's original plans would have seen Hampton Court almost entirely rebuilt had they been executed. In the end however Wren had to draw his horns in, and his work, most arrestingly in the regal Fountain Court, served in fact to extend and embellish and illumine the already magnificent structure.

The marriage of architectural styles in Hampton Court Palace is one of its attractions, echoing in concrete form the liveliness of its history. The particular affection the public has for this palace is surely a consequence of the colour and vivacity of the lives which have been lived here, most impressively of course the life of Henry VIII. For the mention of Hampton Court cannot but summon up in our minds a vision of rust-red brick and Tudor chimneys; of the blood in the cheeks of the young Renaissance Prince, the most gifted man ever to occupy the throne, and the choler in the countenance of the terrible, terrifying old man into which he grew. But if Henry's is the presiding spirit of the place, that of his gleaming adviser, Cardinal Wolsey, is also incontrovertibly present. If the Palace which Wolsey handed over lock, stock and barrel to his King is no longer recognisable, there is no question that Wolsey was a principal progenitor of the kind of magnificence which Hampton Court expresses. Wolsey's Closet (for me one of the most enduring memories of the whole place) is immediately recognisable as a room, a chamber, appropriate to that extraordinary representative of Renaissance splendour.

It is one of the comforting and pleasing qualities of June Osborne's precise and engaging book that she has chosen to be a guide into the historical conundrums of this protean and endlessly fascinating palace. Through a vivid eye she has developed a form of historical reconstruction which helps us understand the men and women whose home Hampton Court has been. It is a consequence of human activity that our interest is engaged. We are reminded of the original house occupied by the Knights Hospitallers, we might imagine, having the austerity of a truly pious establishment. The range and reach of incident, thus concentrated, is very surprising: John Milton, blind genius of *Paradise Lost*, playing the organ to Oliver Cromwell, regicide; the young Princess Elizabeth, temporarily imprisoned here not long before her unanimously supported ascension to the throne; Charles I escaping down the back stairs, scurrying through the 'Paradise Room', on his way to the Isle of Wight in the winter of 1647. From the 280 rooms Wolsey kept permanently prepared for house guests to the less ostentatious but equally magnificent court of the serious-minded William III and of the keen-eyed if short-sighted Queen Mary II, Hampton Court has always provided a stage for the exposition of human character; and Mrs Osborne has understood that it is the evidence of human frailty and human strength that makes this many-sided palace so especially enjoyable.

This book does proper justice to the liveliness of the lives lived and ended at this central cog in the history of the nation. Mrs Osborne has approached her subject with a due respect, and has avoided the conceits of cleverness, allowing the place to speak, as it were, for itself. Her researches have obviously been careful, but the economy of her prose and her affectionate concern to paint a true portrait never allow pedantry or mannerism to complicate the text. As I have suggested, it seems to me that the real quality of this book lies in the author's ability to present Hampton Court Palace as the monument to human nature — greedy, glorious, gleeful and gory — which it unquestionably is. Work such as this helps keep that monument living. As June Osborne writes in the first chapter: "Most people who come to know Hampton Court Palace come to regard it with real affection, and the better they know it the more this affection grows". Hampton Court is regarded with more affection by thousands, possibly millions of people than any other royal palace. This book serves two important purposes germane to that fact: it shows us why this should be so, and it encourages that affection, without affectation, and with engagement.

HUW WHELDON

CHAPTER ONE

Beginnings

"The manor of Hamptone, in the hundred of Spelthorne, . . . is taxed at 35 hides.* The arable land is 25 carucates.† There are 18 hides in demesne, on which are three ploughs. The villeins have 17 ploughs, and 5 more might be employed. There are 30 villeins, who hold each a virgate;‡ 11 villeins who have two hides and a half jointly; and 4 borders, who have half a virgate each."

Trans. Domesday Book. Vol. I Folio 130

Of all the qualities that Hampton Court Palace possesses, perhaps the greatest is this; that it is all things to all people. No one is too old, too young, too unlettered or too learned that they will not derive pleasure from it. It has something for everybody. Most people who know it come to regard it with real affection, and the better they know it the more this affection grows. Since it was first opened to the public early in the reign of Queen Victoria, many quite ordinary people have come to regard it as *their* palace, *their* especial heritage.

It is not only the varied styles of architecture that give the Palace this fascination, the fact that three different periods of building can be recognized, not only the variety of things to see – the state-rooms, the superb art collection, the incomparable gardens, the Maze, the Royal Tennis Court, the Great Vine, the kitchens and cellars. It is also the sense of freedom – you may wander round the grounds at will – and the sense of history.

The Palace has most to offer to those who know something about the events that occurred within its walls. So much of British history did actually happen here. Wolsey entertained the King and Queen here, as well as foreign ambassadors, with much magnificence; here the Cardinal's death was announced to Henry VIII. Here the King's only legitimate son Edward was born and was christened in the Chapel, here Jane Seymour the boy's

11

* "hide" – measure of about 100 acres
† "carucate" – as much land as could be tilled with one plough and eight oxen in a year
‡ "virgate" – about 30 acres

mother, died. Hampton Court saw the first public appearance of Catherine Howard as queen, and fifteen months later her arrest for infidelity, then in 1543 Henry's marriage with his last wife Catherine Parr. Within these rooms Mary Tudor shut herself away to be delivered of a child that was never born; here, almost certainly, Shakespeare acted before James I and the King of Denmark. Here Charles I was held captive, and escaped, here the poet John Milton played the organ to Oliver Cromwell. In Home Park to the east, William III suffered his fatal fall from his horse. In Hampton Court Palace George I entertained his ugly German mistresses, and George II boxed the ears of his royal grandson. Here, in the Grace and Favour apartments, lived the Duke of Wellington's mother and, later, Lady Baden-Powell. Here as recently as November 1982 the British and Dutch royal families joined together for a banquet.

Is it to be wondered then that a palace that has seen so much history has an atmosphere? It is credited with various ghosts. But despite the size and magnificence of the place – it is said to contain 1,100 rooms – it is not daunting but retains a human, almost intimate character.

Thirteen miles from central London, Hampton Court Palace lies on flat, naturally rather open land on the north bank of the Thames. The grounds extend some 1,900 acres, including the western end of Bushey Park from which it is separated – as it has been for perhaps a thousand years – by the ancient highway running from Kingston to the west. This is the approach used today by most motor traffic to the Palace. Equally, it may be reached by rail from Waterloo. But before the road to the north was made up, it was rutted and unsafe, notoriously infested with footpads, and for centuries the river was the preferred means of access.

The name Hampton Court is derived from the Saxon – not surprisingly, since it is barely two miles from Kingston, the crowning-place of most of the Saxon kings. The "Ham" part of the word means a place of shelter or a home, and the "ton" a collection of houses, fortified with hedge and ditch. "Court" did not originally signify any royal connections, for the name is much older than the palace, but rather that the buildings were grouped around a central yard.

A few relics remain as evidence that the place was inhabited from very early times. A hollowed-out tree-trunk canoe (now in the British Museum), and old oak piles that have been found in the river-bed, suggest that this stretch of river was used by the ancient Britons. Roman urns and coins have also been dug up. But the first written mention that we have is in the Domesday Book of 1086, where it is stated that "Hamntone" in the County of Middlesex and the hundred of Spelthorne had in Saxon times belonged to Earl Algar, but now (in Norman times) belonged to Walter de St Valerie or Valeric. It included arable land and cattle pasture, and its total value was put at the comparatively high figure of £39, including three shillings from fisheries in the River Thames.

The manor of Hampton Court remained in the hands of the St Valerie family until the early thirteenth century. Thomas de St Valery, the owner at that time, rebelled against the King and had all his other lands confiscated by Henry III. Hampton Court, however, he had already given away to Henry de St Albans – who in his turn seems, in 1236, to have given or leased it to the Knights Hospitallers of St John of Jerusalem. And despite the efforts of his grand-daughters and co-heiresses Sabrina de Dunholm, or Durham, and Joan Lady de Grey to get it back, it remained their property until the sixteenth century.

Who were these Knights Hospitallers? They were a crusading order, and were established in 1113 to look after sick and poor pilgrims; this was the aspect of their work emphasized by their first Master, Gerard. But then they became a more military and international organization, and came to rival the Templars in wealth and power. By the late thirteenth century their centre was moved to Rhodes, then in 1530 to Malta – after this they became known as the Knights of Malta. Their badge was first a simple cross, then after about 1350 a Maltese cross.

At Hampton Court they had a manor-house with a small chapel, barns and outbuildings, all probably built around a central courtyard; there was also a garden with a dovecote. The estates were used for farming, both arable and pasture – they kept about 2,000 sheep. They also fished in the River Thames, did their own brewing and baking, and the profits from the estate went to the funds of their Order. They also provided a place of retreat. In February 1503 Henry VII's devout wife Elizabeth of York came here for this purpose. She travelled by boat from Richmond Palace, shortly before her seventh and last child was born, and prayed for a safe delivery. Her prayers went unanswered and a month later she died in childbirth.

Very little now remains of the Knights Hospitallers' manor-house, and it is difficult to picture what it looked like. In 1514 the contents were listed – the furnishings seem fairly sparse. There were only two chairs, though 22 bedsteads; there was a trestle table of "Estriche bourde" and a "parclose" (partition screen) in the parlour, two "dormant" tables and a long trestle table in the hall, also a "close cupbourde", four forms and four "barres of yron about the harthe". A press and a great coffer, as well as another parclose, were found in the tower-chambers. In the stable, a pitchfork and a dungfork.

The kitchen was more generously suppled with: "a pot of bras cont v galons, a cadron [cauldron] sett in the fournace cont xx galons, a spyt of yron, ij awndyrons [andirons], a trevet, ij morters of marbil, a cawdron of iij galons di. a stomer [steamer] of laton [brass], a flesshehoke, a frying pan, ij pailes, a barre of yron in the kechen to hang on pottes, a grete salting troghe, a steping fatte, an heire of the kyln of xxiij yerdes, ij grete bynnes in the kechen, a bynne in the buttry, a knedyng troghe."

The provision of a great salting trough reminds us of the need at the time to salt down enough meat to last the winter.

Meanwhile the chapel was furnished with such things as a silver chalice, a copper pyx, various altarcloths including one patterned in blue and white, two latten [brass] candlesticks, a missal, a pewter bottle for wine, a pewter cruet, a wooden paten, wooden figures of Christ and the Virgin, an image of St Nicholas, and "an ymage of the crosse paynted on a borde". The list of chapel furnishings ends with "ij bells in the towre, one of them broken."

From the manor-house of the Knights Hospitallers there survives today only one bell, possibly some masonry, a Maltese cross in the paving of Clock Court, and some fifteenth-century painting in the room known as Wolsey's Closet. In the 1960s the sixteenth-century panels there which depict the Passion and form a frieze above the linenfold panelling were cleaned, and it was found that under at least part of them was earlier painting of very fine quality. This must date back to the days of the Knights Hospitallers.

But apart from this, virtually all the manor-house was surely destroyed by Cardinal Wolsey when, early in the reign of Henry VIII, he decided to build at Hampton Court a palace far grander than anything the King possessed.

CHAPTER TWO

Wolsey's Rise

"A great carle he is and fatt,
Wearing on his head a red hatt."
the monk Roy

Thomas Wolsey was born at Ipswich in about 1473, the son of
Robert Wolsey, a grazier and innkeeper. From these modest
beginnings he rose to power in what was almost the only way
open to him, through scholarship and the Church. He was edu-
cated at Oxford and became a Fellow of Magdalen College, where
he taught until 1500. Then he obtained his first living at Liming-
ton, Somerset, and by the following year was chaplain to Deane,
Archbishop of Canterbury.

It was doubtless through his standing with the Archbishop
that he became a royal chaplain six years later, and as such
became involved in diplomatic affairs. By 1511 he was promoted
to almoner and councillor, and helped in the following year to
organize the expedition against the French made by Henry VIII
and Maximilian I, head of the Holy Roman Empire. This expedition culminated in the Battle of the Spurs, by which they gained
possession of Thérouanne and Tournai, and as a reward for his
services Wolsey was afterwards made Bishop of Tournai. He
became Dean of St Stephen's Westminster and Precentor of St
Paul's. In 1514 he was also created Bishop of Lincoln, then Archbishop of York. By then he had become so indispensable to the
King, who in his twenties cared little for the business of government, that he was made Lord Chancellor – succeeding William
Warham, who became Archbishop of Canterbury. Wolsey promptly dissolved parliament, and did not summon it again until
eight years later.

Later, in 1515, on 10th September, Pope Leo X was persuaded
by a letter, which came ostensibly from the King but was probably drafted by the candidate himself, to make Wolsey a cardinal.

The letter described him as "our most secret counsellor" and declared that he, the king, could take no important decision without him.

The final accolade came in 1518 when Wolsey was made a legate *a latere* – that is to say, the representative of the pontificate within this country. This gave him supremacy over all the clergy, including the Archbishop of Canterbury. When the two were in procession together, Wolsey took precedence and had two crosses as well as two silver pillars and two pole-axes borne in front of him; Archbishop Warham was not allowed even one cross. With Henry's encouragement, attempts were made in 1521 and again in 1523 to have Wolsey elected Pope. Emperor Charles V (who had succeeded Maximilian) was against him, so he did not succeed, but the very fact that his name was twice put forward indicated that here was no ordinary man.

There was nothing saintly about him. He used his position in the Church as a means of gaining temporal power: he certainly had no vocation for it. He kept a mistress and had a son and daughter by her: the girl became a nun, and the boy, who was called Thomas Wynter, gained through nepotism preferment in the Church. Wolsey was extremely loyal to King Henry and cared little for the option of anyone else. Though ruthless, proud, extravagant, he was to some extent the champion of the poor, whose causes he heard, with surprising sympathy, in the Court of the Star Chamber. He also gave considerable sums to finance Cardinal College (now Christ Church College), Oxford. Another point in his favour was that during his supremacy no heretics were burnt. He was not liked so much as admired. The Venetian ambassador, Sebastiano Giustiani, said of him "he is very handsome, learned, extremely eloquent, and indefatigable. He alone transacts the same business which occupies all the magistracies, offices and councils of Venice, both civil and criminal: and all state affairs are managed by him . . . he is in very great repute – seven times more than if he were Pope."

With this extraordinary power – surely never equalled by any commoner – came incredible wealth. An unrepentant pluralist, he enjoyed the stipends of all his various offices in the Church

17

simultaneously. As Lord High Chancellor he accepted commissions wherever he granted requests, he appropriated probate fees of a shilling in the pound on all wills, and in his dealings with foreign powers seldom failed to turn the transactions to his financial advantage. From France alone, for instance, he received a pension of 25,000 crowns "without the extras".*

Loving ostentation, Wolsey flaunted his riches. Wherever he was, according to Giustiani, "he had a sideboard of plate worth 25,000 ducats". To the Field of Cloth of Gold in 1520 he brought with him 50 gentlemen, 12 chaplains and 237 servants – only the King had a larger suite. As for Hampton Court, his annual household expenses there must have amounted to the equivalent of at least £5 million in modern money, and at his palace of York Place (later called Whitehall) probably even more. Wolsey became so accustomed to his splendid mode of living that he came to regard luxuries as necessities, and defended his extravagance thus, "How think ye? were it better for me, being in the honour and dignity that I am, to coin my pillars and pole-axes, and give the money to five or six beggars? Do you not reckon the commonwealth better than five or six beggars?"

In his heyday Wolsey ruled without reference to other ministers and without cabinet to support him: he and they were not allied to each other but bound only to the King. Wolsey summoned parliament only once during his fourteen years of power, and according to Sir Thomas More (1518) settled affairs himself first and only consulted the council afterwards. Giustiani, the Venetian ambassador, succinctly expressed Wolsey's phenomenal rise to power: when he, Giustiani, first arrived in England in 1515, Wolsey would say to him, "His Majesty will do so and so." Later he would say, "We shall do so and so." But at present, he wrote in 1519, "he has reached such a pitch that he says, 'I shall do so and so.'" Or in the words of Shakespeare, "ego et rex meus": "I and my king".

Vigorous, Wolsey certainly was, but he was a moody man, and his moods largely depended on his health. He was never robust and suffered periodically from digestive complaints, also dropsy and fevers of various kinds including the sweating sick-

* Chapuys, 31st December 1529

ness so prevalent in Tudor times. It is said that he chose Hampton Court as the site for his new palace because of the nearby springs of sweet water at Coombe. Rightly he preferred them to the polluted Thames and had them tapped, but it was probably unfortunate that the water was conveyed through leaden pipes. The pipes, $2\frac{1}{2}$ inches in diameter, were laid in 25-foot lengths carefully joined together, over the distance of some 3 miles. The effluent was taken away from the palace by great brick sewers, measuring 3 feet by 5 feet in section, and deposited in the Thames. Such sanitary provisions were most unusual in the sixteenth century; whether or not the story is true that Wolsey directed his physicians to find him the most salubrious site within twenty miles of London, the fact remains that Hampton Court was a comparatively healthy place, easy of access by river, and altogether a wise choice.

Wolsey, then Archbishop of York but not yet Cardinal, acquired it from the Knights Hospitallers of St John on 11th January 1514. He was not able to buy it, as he would no doubt have wished, but only to rent it on a 99-year lease for the very reasonable sum of £50 a year. Out of this, £4. 13s. 4d. was set aside to pay for a priest to say services in the chapel. At the same time the Prior and his knights granted Wolsey four loads of wood each year in order to repair the weir, for there was no bridge at this point until the mid-eighteenth century. The Archbishop and his assignees undertook to keep the warren well-stocked with rabbits, but they were free to make tremendous changes to the buildings, "at all tymes" to "take down, alter, transpose, change, make new byeld at theire propre costs any houses, walles, mootes, diches, warkis, or other things within or about the said manour . . . without any payne or punysshment." Of this licence Wolsey took full advantage, and set about erecting a palace which would epitomize his power and wealth.

The plans are said to have been drawn up by a man called Ellis Smith,* and in the spring of 1515 a great moat was dug to encircle the building. The course of this moat can clearly be seen today, on the west side of the Palace, and a recent excavation in Lady Mornington's Garden, on the east side, has revealed how

---

* Other names have also been suggested. Law quotes a manuscript giving the name of James Bettes as "master of the works", Nicholas Townley as "clerk controller".

Terracotta Roundel of the Emperor Augustus, by Giovanni da Maiano, situated in Clock Court.

the sloping walls there had been used later as a foundation for Anne Boleyn's Gallery. Within its circumference Wolsey had created a herb garden, planted with thyme, parsley, caraway and such. Eightpence was paid for a butt to supply water for the herbs, and the accounts also include the item of twelve pence paid to a woman called Agnes "for 4 days wedinge in my lorde's garthing and orchard at 3*d*. the day".

It is hard to say whether anything remains of the structure of the Knights Hospitallers' manor-house. It is possible that some of its masonry may have been "cannibalized"; this was common practice at the time. Wolsey set to, and ordered supplies: the red bricks with which his palace was mainly built were made by the firm of Richard Reculver at a cost of three shillings a thousand. The stone, used for decorative details including heraldic beasts and gargoyles, was brought from Reigate and Barnet, and lime for the mortar from Ruislip.

Wolsey's palace was built around three principal courtyards — the Base Court (which still exists), the adjoining one now known as Clock Court (considerably altered at various times) and another court to the east, formerly known as Cloister Green and rebuilt by Wren to form the present Fountain Court. Wolsey began building with the west front and made the main approach through the Great Gatehouse, then two storeys higher than it is today. The predominating red brick was enhanced with diamond patterns in bluish black. The whole edifice was crowned with numerous turrets, each one capped with a leaden cupola. At this time were set up the decorative chimneys (such a distinctive feature of the palace), although most of them have now been rebuilt. The exterior of the palace was further adorned with his coat-of-arms and a set of terracotta roundels, originally coloured, and depicting the Roman emperors. These were commissioned from Giovanni da Maiano, who came from Florence in 1521, and made them at a cost of £2. 6*s*. 8*d*. apiece. There is an old story that they were a gift from the Pope: in any case they were among the first works of Italian Renaissance art to be seen in this country.

For Wolsey's recreation was made a long window-lit gallery

and, in the garden, an arbour where he frequently would sit in the evenings. Stabling was built to the west, and the park south of the Hampton-Kingston road enclosed with the brick wall that, apart from repairs, still exists.

Altogether Wolsey's palace must have occupied nearly the eight acres taken up by the building as it stands today. It contained about a thousand rooms. Something of their grandeur can be judged by what survives today, in particular the ceiling in what is known as Wolsey's Closet: intricate plasterwork picked out in colours and gold, and bordered with the Cardinal's motto *"Dominus Mihi Adjutor"*, (God is, or God be, my Judge). Two hundred and eighty rooms were always made ready for guests.

In all, Wolsey employed a staff of about five hundred people, varying greatly in status and function. There were fifty priests who walked before him in procession, a dean and sub-dean, a repeater of the choir, priests to sing the gospel and epistle at High Mass, sixteen singing laymen, (the number was sometimes augmented), and twelve singing boys. His household was controlled by the high chamberlain, under him the vice-chamberlain, and it included gentleman ushers, yeoman ushers, waiters, cupbearers, carvers and grooms of the chamber. There were sixteen doctors, four lawyers, three clerks and two secretaries. As Lord Chamberlain, Wolsey employed more clerks, also footmen, armourers, serjeants-at-arms, heralds and minstrels. All these mouths had to be fed. There were two kitchens under the direction of his master-cook, who sat dressed in satin and velvet issuing orders to his subordinates: assistant cooks, grooms, bakers, servants of the saucery, buttery, ewery, scalding-house, pastry-house and scullery. More servants were employed looking after clothes, laundering, sewing, caring for the horses and the Cardinal's grey and white mules, fetching wood and drawing water. Two yeomen and two grooms were stationed at the porters' lodge.

In short, the Cardinal kept his own court, quite distinct from the King's. The two had their own preoccupations and spent little time together: their contact was nearly all through correspondence. Whenever his official duties permitted him (for during

The Wolsey Closet.
Above the linenfold panelling, the 16th-century painted panels show the Last Supper and the story of the Passion. The richly plastered ceiling bordered with Wolsey's motto survives to indicate the splendour of his Palace.

the legal terms he had to attend sessions daily in Westminster Hall), Wolsey would leave London. He had properties at Tittenhanger in Bedfordshire and The More in Hertfordshire, but Hampton Court was close enough to London to enable him to transact state affairs. There he rose early, said two masses, dealt with his private business affairs and had breakfast, all before eight o'clock. Then he emerged dressed in his scarlet cardinal's robes, made of the richest materials and cut according to the patterns worn by the cardinals of the Curia in Rome; round his neck he would wear a stole of the finest sables. Thus arrayed he would give audiences and receive those visitors fortunate enough to obtain access, issue orders to his agents abroad, read, write, sign documents and take decisions. Little time was left for relaxation. Occasionally Wolsey went hunting with the King, more often he walked in the galleries or sat outside among the knot-gardens.

The interior of the Palace was furnished as lavishly as this way of life suggests. The two hundred and eighty guest beds were equipped with curtains, bedspreads and canopies, all in the richest materials, for instance:
"A new bed, paned with crimson tinsell satin, fringed with red russet silk and Venice gold, the celar [canopy] thereof with valances, and fine curtains of red and russet sarcanet."

For Wolsey's own bed there were soft wool mattresses, fine white blankets trimmed with lamb's fur, quilts of red silk or of "sarcanet paned white and green, with my Lord's arms and a crown of Thorn in the midst", pillowcases "seamed with black silk and fleur-de-lys of gold", or with "white silk and fleur-de-lys of red silk".

The Chapel, which he may have rebuilt sometime before 1525, was now lavishly furnished with rich jewels and ornaments, images of saints and fine clothes of cloth of gold and damask to put on them, chalices and pyxes of gold and silver, numerous copes and other vestments, crosses, candlesticks and bells. This was a far cry from the austerity of the Knights Hospitallers.

Those fortunate enough to possess carpets in the sixteenth century did not generally use them to tread on. It was a mark of Wolsey's wealth that he had carpets of all kinds – "foot-carpets", "table-carpets" and "window-carpets" – some of the more modest wool ones made in England, but the richest silk ones imported by Venetian merchants from Damascus. Sixty such carpets were received from Venice on 24th October 1521.

The rest of the furnishings were similarly magnificent; chairs of state covered in cloth of gold or crimson velvet with red and gold fringes, in black velvet or red leather, and embroidered with Wolsey's coat-of-arms. Then there were tables of cypress or pine, oak cupboards, chests of various sorts, a great number of cushions; and in the many fireplaces were andirons appropriately ornamented with cardinal's hats, dragons, lions, roses and gold balls.

Wolsey's great pride and joy, though, was his collection of tapestries. Many of these were bought or commissioned on his behalf by his agent Sir Richard Gresham. For instance, Gresham bought, in December 1522, a mass order of 132 tapestries (twenty-one sets), and these were used in the rooms of the Great Gatehouse. Many of the tapestries acquired for the Cardinal were of religious subjects, as might seem appropriate, but there were also heraldic borders specially made with his own coat-of-arms, and secular subjects. These included a set of Triumphs, made in Flanders and based on the works of Petrarch – Triumphs of Death, Time, Fame, Chastity, Love and Eternity – some of which are still to be seen in the Palace, mainly in the Great Watching Chamber. In Wolsey's own bedroom he had, perhaps to caution him, tapestries illustrating the Seven Deadly Sins.

In such a setting Wolsey entertained lavishly and at huge expense. Always at the centre of European diplomacy, he took it on himself to receive foreign ambassadors amongst his other guests. As his sixteenth-century biographer, Cavendish, expressed it,*

"His house was always resorted to and furnished with noblemen, gentlemen, and other persons, with going and coming in and out, feasting and banquetting all ambassadors divers times, and other strangers right nobly."

The King and Queen Catherine of Aragon were entertained too, and must have been among his first guests when they came there in May 1516, the palace still incomplete. Wolsey would sit at the centre of the high table, in a banqueting hall decked with great vases of gold and silver, and after the meal there were masquerades in which the nobility as well as the professionals took part. At one of them were "thirty-six masquers disguised, all in one suite of fine green satin, all overcovered with cloth of gold, and masking hoods on their heads: the ladies had tyers made of braids of damask gold, with long hairs of white gold. All these masquers danced at one time, and after they had danced they put off then visors, and they they were all known."

Next, a light supper was served, followed by gambling with dice, and dancing far into the night.

* *Life of Wolsey*, Vol. II, p. 112

Wolsey's coat-of-arms over the Anne Boleyn Gateway in Clock Court. Made in terracotta, and surmounted by his cardinal's hat, it is surprising that Henry VIII did not destroy it altogether when he took over the Palace.

Wolsey's way of life was in short hardly what one would expect of a churchman. He may have kept in his bedroom a tapestry reminding him of the deadly sin of pride, but the warning went unheeded. When he rode in processions it was on a mule, by tradition a humble beast, but the Cardinal's mule was carefully groomed, caparisoned in crimson velvet, and carried stirrups of gilded copper.

When Wolsey's famous hat first arrived from Rome it was brought by a protonotary from the Curia, who on landing was given a change of sumptuous clothing. The hat was taken to Blackheath, where it was met by a bishop and an earl. Then the mayor, aldermen and city guilds of London formed a procession to carry the hat to Westminster, where it was laid on the high altar in the Abbey. Three archbishops, eight bishops and eight abbots took part in a mass to celebrate its arrival; "I have not seen the like," wrote Cavendish, "unless it hath bin at the coronation of a mighty prince."

25

With so much ceremony just in honour of his hat, and its wearer not even present, it follows that even greater attended the Cardinal himself. He was notoriously difficult to approach. "No one obtains audience from him unless at the third or fourth attempt." declared Giustiani, "I have been several times to the right reverend Cardinal but could never obtain audience: true it is that he was always occupied, either with the ambassadors [of Spain] or those of France, so that there was no room for me." Wolsey was, of course, a very busy man; having so many different matters to attend to, he could hardly have been otherwise. But he was also overbearing, peremptory and at times downright bad-tempered. He is said to have seized the Papal Nuncio and threatened him with the rack if he did not reveal what had been negotiated with the French. If a courtier was lucky enough to obtain an audience with Wolsey, he had to pass through a series of eight presence-chambers, hung with tapestries all the way along – and Wolsey had so many tapestries that they were changed round every week – and there at the end would be the great Cardinal, sitting in state. At dinner in the Great Hall, it seems, Wolsey would sit alone under a golden canopy and was not only served first, but had to have finished his meal before anyone else was even allowed to begin.

A summons from Wolsey was like a royal command. "Omnipotent", Erasmus called him. And the grandeur of his palace at Hampton Court was the supreme expression of his power and pride,

> *"More lyke unto a paradice*
> *Than any earthly habitation."*
>
> (Roy)

CHAPTER THREE

Wolsey's Downfall

"Whosoever shall exalt himself shall be abased,
and he that shall humble himself shall be exalted."

This was the text of the sermon preached by Colet, Dean of St Paul's, at the service held in Westminster Abbey in honour of Wolsey's hat. It was brave of the Dean, for at this time – however many men nursed secret grudges – there was hardly a word spoken openly against the Cardinal. Colet's words were also prophetic of Wolsey's ultimate downfall.

The Cardinal's eminent position relied solely on the support of the King. Especially in his youth, Henry disliked paperwork. The elder statesmen, Foxe and Warham, were for ever exhorting him to be a little more like his father, Henry VII, who attended regularly at the Council table, and checked every page of the palace accounts. But the young king was a very different character, and it was understandable that he favoured Wolsey who cheerfully offered to shoulder the burden of administration for him, and instead of nagging him encouraged the King to follow his own pursuits. Meanwhile Wolsey loved to entertain the King with masques and feasting. "This was his only study", wrote Cavendish, "to devise things for His Majesty's comfort, not weighing the charges or expenses."

As Wolsey grew in temporal power, in international as well as English affairs, he was simultaneously raised to higher and higher rank in the Church. Consequently a strong bond was forged with the Vatican; as the Bishop of Durham declared to a Venetian ambassador as early as 1515, "The pope is now so linked with the king that words cannot exaggerate their mutual goodwill; so that, in the affairs of France, the policy of England will be that of Rome." And the King, to his delight, was given for the first time the title "*Fidei Defensor*" – Defender of the Faith.

This was all very fine as long as the Pope, the King and Wolsey remained in agreement and had no conflicting objectives in view. But power which depends on the favour of one man is inevitably precarious, and Wolsey's position as papal legate did nothing to stabilize it. Rather the reverse, it alienated him from the rest of the clergy. There were two sorts of papal legate, *natus* and *a latere*. Warham was *legatus natus* by virtue of his being Archbishop of Canterbury, (so indeed was Wolsey when he became Archbishop of York; the status went with the office), but a *legatus natus* was still subject to the ruler of his country. A *legatus a latere*, on the other hand, was normally a foreigner, sent by the Curia for some specific purpose, holding great power in that one respect, but only for a limited period. Wolsey was an exception; there was no such specific purpose, and he was supposed to hold the office for life. He never once went to Rome, although he went through the charade of pretending that he had; he would disappear for a few days and then emerge with a directive which he claimed came straight from the Pope. He had complete sway and the government of the Church was, in short, controlled by this one legate and not by convocation.

Clergy were usually appointed by acclamation rather than election. Fees were charged for visitations made to religious establishments by Wolsey's representatives: and they were also charged to individual members of the clergy when they were offered livings. All these went into the Cardinal's pocket. In the diocese of Canterbury, Wolsey was particularly disliked because he overrode the sway of the Archbishop who was normally considered to be the Primate of the land; but the feeling was also general, and the more he exercised his special powers as legate the more unpopular he became.

It was not only in the Church that there was this growing hatred. He was a complete autocrat amd his combination of high offices was quite without precedent. Nor did he carry his power gracefully. His stage management of the Field of Cloth of Gold seems to have been performed mainly for reasons of self-aggrandizement. When in 1518 Cardinal Campeggio was sent by Pope Leo X, Wolsey kept him hanging about in Calais for two months until he too was made a legate. In 1519 he replaced the lively, frivolous and Francophile ''young minions'' who danced attendance on the king, with ''four sad and ancient knights'', and this no doubt antagonized some of the younger aristocracy. But what must have annoyed almost everyone who tried to approach him was his aloofness. Thomas Allen, writing to the Earl of Shrewsbury, complained,

''When he walks in the park he will suffer no suitor to come near, but commands them off, as far as a man can shoot an arrow.''

Wolsey disliked London, but when he had to go into crowded places it was his habit to carry a pomander. This was an orange with the flesh taken out and replaced with herbs, spices and vinegar, which he held up to his nose to guard against ''the pestilent airs''.

Perhaps the unwisest thing that Wolsey ever did was to incur the hatred of Anne Boleyn – whose influence over the King he gravely underestimated.

Anne Boleyn had been in France in the Court of Queen Claude, first wife of François I, but came back to England in 1522 when there was a threat of another war against the French. Among her suitors at that time was Sir Henry Percy, heir to the Earl of Northumberland and a protégé of Wolsey's. Despite his interest in Anne, he was already engaged to Lady Mary Talbot. Percy asked Wolsey if this engagement could be broken so that he would be free to marry Anne, who seems to have been equally in love with him. Wolsey, perhaps realizing that Anne had already attracted the King's attention, refused to encourage this idea, and finally had the young man sent back to Northumberland.

Wolsey's motives in this affair seem to have been fairly altruistic – he was working on the King's behalf rather than his own – but Anne never forgave him. She was sent away from the Court, back to her father's house at Hever in Kent, (''whereat she smoked'', wrote Wolsey's biographer Cavendish). The animosity between them grew; Wolsey called her a wicked woman and a ''night crow'', and Anne secretly planned to revenge herself in whatever way she could.

Whatever her feeling may have been for him, the King was

undoubtedly deeply in love with Anne. Between 1527 and 1528 he wrote her a series of love-letters:

"I would you were in my arms, or I in yours, for I think it long since I kissed you. Written . . . by the hand which I trust shortly shall be yours, Henry R."

The courtship was prolonged, for Anne – unlike her sister Mary who had been the King's mistress – held out for marriage or nothing. It was not only, however, his passion for her that motivated Henry in what became known as "The King's Great Matter". He was also concerned about the succession, because his first wife Catherine of Aragon had failed to provide him with a living male heir. Her sons were born dead or died soon after, the only surviving child being his daughter Mary. The only precedent for a queen ruling in her own right in this country was the rather unhappy one of Matilda, rival to King Stephen, so Henry feared that if no legitimate son were born to him England might be plunged into civil war. He began to question, therefore, the validity of his marriage to Catherine. She had been married before – very young, as was the custom – to his short-lived elder brother Arthur. Though she maintained that she had never slept with him, it had been necessary to seek a papal dispensation before she could be wedded to his brother. Henry now began to cast doubts on whether the Pope had had the right to give this dispensation, in view of the text from Leviticus (*Chapter XX, v.21*):

"If a man shall take his brother's wife, it is an unclean thing: he hath uncovered his brother's nakedness; they shall be childless."

Henry may have genuinely believed that this was the reason for the deaths of all but one of his children. He sought the Cardinal's aid to annul his marriage.

Wolsey was in a difficult position. He had, it is true, never been on very good terms with Catherine, who disapproved of his keeping a mistress and felt he allied himself too much with Francis I and too little with her nephew, Charles V. Moreover he dared not oppose the King on whose favour he depended. Therefore Wolsey had no reason to oppose the divorce as such and, had Henry been willing to agree to the match with Renée of France which the Cardinal was trying to put forward as an alternative, he could have supported it whole-heartedly, and might have held on to his power and possessions. But the King's mind was set on Anne and no one else. The Cardinal went down on his knees but failed to dissuade him. Wolsey dreaded the idea of Anne becoming queen; Henry suspected that Wolsey was not working on his behalf with as much assiduity as he might have, and possibly was double-dealing and secretly supporting Catherine. And so, it was commented by the Spanish ambassador, "the cardinal is no longer received at court so graciously as before."

Thus it was that Wolsey's critics began to come out into the open and castigate him for his extravagant way of life. Among the most vociferous was John Skelton, who took him to task not only for his secular wall-hangings, not only about his diet and his eating pork and poultry in Lent, but also for his magnificent palace at Hampton Court. "Why come ye not to Court?" he wrote in verses possibly directed to Archbishop Warham,

> "Why come ye not to Court?
> To which Court?
> To the King's Court
> Or to Hampton Court?
> Nay, to the King's Court!
> The King's Court
> Should hath the excellence
> But Hampton Court
> Hath the pre-eminence."

This was published in 1523: Skelton had perhaps gone a little too far, or spoken a little too soon, and he was forced to seek sanctuary at Westminster.

Wolsey's autocracy and ostentation were widely criticized: "Have they not in Englonde a kinge?" questioned the Franciscan monk Roy. An anonymous ballad circulating in 1528 urged Wolsey to live more modestly,

> "And do like the peacock for thine avail,

31

> Look on thy feet and down with thy tail,
> And off with thy golden shoon!
> And lay down thy pillars, poleaxes and crosses,
> By which this land hath had great losses
> And pill the people no more!''

Tyndale (the translator of the Bible) and Foxe (the writer of the *Book of Martyrs*) added their weight to such opinions. Tyndale condemned his frivolity: ''A gay finder-out of new pastimes'' he called him, and the King himself criticized Wolsey's way of extorting money when he visited religious houses:
''Surely this can hardly be with good conscience. For, and they were good, why should you take money? and if they were ill, it were a sinful act.''

Wolsey was forgiven on this occasion, but he was still anxious as to whether he could retain Henry's favour. There is a story, which may or may not be true, that the King demanded to know of Wolsey, ''Why he had built so magnificent a house for himself at Hampton Court'', and Wolsey was swift to reply, ''To show how noble a palace a subject may offer to his sovereign.'' It is certain that by 1525 he had handed the ownership of the Palace to the King, doubtless in an attempt to regain his favour. According to Cavendish (who as Wolsey's gentleman-usher might be expected to know), it was given in exchange for a house at Richmond. A letter from Jehan le Sauche dated 25th June 1525 comments on the Cardinal's surrender of the Palace, ''Henceforth he will lodge as any other of the King's servants. *Il me semble que l'on appelle cela :'Je vous donne un cochon de vostre pourcheau au grant merchys du vostre.'''* (I give you a pig from your own sty at your own great expense).

Wolsey's palace was at this time only just completed. Although it now officially belonged to the King, Wolsey continued to live there for the next three years. It was at this time that the rooms called ''The Wolsey Rooms'' (probably used for guests before), became known as ''My Lord Cardinal's Lodgings'', which suggests that this is where he himself resided. Apart from that, his way of life seems to have continued to be as extravagant as before. When he wrote letters to the King he generally remembered to refer to the Palace as "Your Grace's manor of Hampton Court"; but as far as everyone else was concerned, it was still his house. Wolsey was still trusted to act on the King's behalf and negotiate with the French.

At Hampton Court on 8th August 1526 he and the French ambassador signed an alliance, undertaking that neither Henry VIII nor Francis I should join with Charles V in opposition to the other, and that Henry should do what he could towards the liberation of the French king's sons.* Then Wolsey received the Venetian ambassadors also at Hampton Court, and in the following year representatives from France arrived to negotiate an even closer alliance between the two countries. In particular they wished to arrange a marriage (which never came off) between Francis I and Henry's ten-year-old daughter Mary. On this occasion both Henry and Catherine of Aragon (and very likely Mary too) were at the Palace. The ambassadors were first greeted by Wolsey and presented by him to the King, then after dinner the whole party adjourned to the Queen's chamber (according to Law, her rooms were on the first floor on the east side of what is now Clock Court). But the business side of the meeting appears to have been left to Wolsey; the French envoy found him wily and resolute – "We have to deal with the most rascally beggar in the world," he wrote to Francis, "and one who is wholly devoted to his master's interests – a man as difficult to manage as can be!" Wolsey's will prevailed. A treaty was drawn up directing that the French should pay over an annual tribute in salt and in money (50,000 crowns) and a lump sum of about 2 million crowns, payable by instalments. Although these clauses were ratified in Amiens, when Wolsey went to France in September 1527 to meet Francis I, they were drawn up at the Palace and became known as the Treaty of Hampton Court. Henry VIII was to be invested with the Order of St Michael, and for this purpose a great embassy came to England. It consisted of French nobles, clergy and dignitaries, accompanied by captains of the guard and five or six hundred horsemen. At first they were lodged in the City of London at the expense of the Mayor and burgesses, then

33

* The Dauphin and the Duke of Orléans had been taken as hostage to Spain in exchange for their father's freedom, and were living in a wretched dark prison furnished only with a straw mattress.

they moved to Greenwich for the actual investiture, which took place in the old Palace of Placentia. A mass was sung in St Paul's Cathedral, and the Cardinal entertained them all to dinner at York Place (later to be known as the Palace of Whitehall).

Then the King himself went back to Greenwich, but arranged for the French gentlemen to spend a little time hunting at Richmond, after which he decided they were to be entertained at Hampton Court, before riding to Windsor and finally returning down river to be feasted at the Court. On this occasion Wolsey seems to have been given little choice over offering hospitality to this great number, so hasty preparations had to be made. As Cavendish recalls,

"There was then no more to do but to make provision at Hampton Court for this assembly in readiness for the day appointed. My Lord called for his principal officers of his house, such as his steward, Comptroller, and the clerks of his kitchen, whom he commanded to prepare for this banquet at Hampton Court; and to spare neither expense nor labour, to make the French such triumphant cheer that they might not only wonder at it here but also make a glorious report in their country, to the King's honour and that of his realm. His pleasure once known, to accomplish his commandment they sent forth all their caterers, purveyors and other persons, to prepare the finest viands that they could get, either for money or friendship, among my Lord's friends. Also they sent for all the expertest cooks, besides my lord's, that they could get in all England . . . to serve to garnish this feast.

"The yeomen and grooms of the wardrobes were busied in hanging the chambers with costly hangings and furnishing the same with beds of silk and other furniture . . . Then my lord Cardinal sent me, being gentleman-usher, with two other of my fellows to Hampton Court, to foresee that everything for which we were accountable was nobly provided. Our pains were not small or light, toiling daily from chamber to chamber. Then the carpenters, the joiners, the masons, the painters, and all other artificers necessary to glorify the house and feast, were set at work. There was carriage and re-carriage of plate, stuff, and other rich implements . . . There were also fourteen score beds provided and furnished with all manner of furniture to them belonging."

The French party arrived earlier than expected at the Palace, so they were sent off to spend the rest of the day hunting at Hanworth, two or three miles away. Then they rode back to Hampton Court,

"and every one of them was conveyed separately to his chamber, where were great fires and wine ready to refresh them. They remained there until their supper was ready and the chambers where they should sup were ordered in due form. The first waiting-chamber was hanged with fine arras, and so was all the rest, one better then another, furnished with tall yeomen. There were set tables round about the chamber, banquet-wise, all covered with fine cloths of diaper, and a cupboard with plate of parcel-gilt. There were also in the same chamber, to give more light, four plates of silver, set with lights upon them, and a great fire in the chimney.

"The next chamber, being the presence chamber, was hung with very rich arras, wherein was a gorgeous and a precious cloth of state hung up, and it was replenished with many goodly gentlemen ready to serve. The boards were set as the other boards were in the other chamber, save that the high table was set apart beneath the cloth of state, towards the midst of the chamber, covered with fine linen cloths of damask work, sweetly perfumed. There was a cupboard made for the occasion, in length of the breadth of the lower end of the same chamber, six shelves high, full of gilt plate, very sumptuous and of the newest fashions. And upon the lowest shelf, garnished all with plate of clean gold, were two great candlesticks of silver and gilt, most curiously wrought (the workmanship whereof, with the silver, cost three hundred marks) and lights of wax as big as torches burning upon the same. This cupboard was barred in round about that no man might come near it; for there was none of the same plate used or stirred during this feast, there being sufficient besides. The plates that hung on the walls to give lights in the chamber were of silver and gilt, with lights burning in them, and a great fire in the chimney and all other things necessary for the furniture of so noble a feast."

The Frenchmen were much impressed and "rapt into a heavenly paradise". However, the Cardinal himself did not appear until after the first course. Then he arrived in his riding clothes, booted and spurred, and bidding them welcome, sat down in their midst.

"Anon came up the second course, with so many dishes, subtleties and curious devices, which were above a hundred in number, of so goodly proportion, and costly, that I suppose the French men never saw the like. There were castles with images in the same; Paul's church and steeple, in proportion for the quantity, as well counterfeited as if the painter should have painted it upon a cloth or wall. There were beasts, birds, fowls of diverse kinds, and personages, most lively made and counterfeit in dishes; some fighting, as it were with swords, some with guns and crossbows, some vaulting and leaping, some dancing with ladies, some in complete harness, jousting with spears. . . . There was a chess-board subtly made of spiced sweetmeat, with men of the same; and for the good proportion, because Frenchmen be very expert in that play, my lord gave the same to a gentleman of France, commanding that a case should be made for the same in all haste, to preserve it from perishing in the conveyance thereof into his country. Then my lord took a bowl of gold, which was esteemed of the value of five hundred marks, and filled it with hippocras, whereof there was plenty, and putting off his cap, said, 'I drink to the King my sovereign lord and master, and the King your master,' and therewith drank a good draught. And when he had done, he desired the Grand Master to pledge him, cup and all, the which cup he gave him; and so caused all the other lords and gentlemen in other cups to pledge these two royal princes."

Meanwhile room-service was being provided:

"And whilst they were in communication . . . all their liveries were served to their chambers. Every chamber had a bason and a ewer of silver, some clear gilt and some parcel gilt; and some two great pots of silver, in like manner, and one pot at the least with wine and beer, a bowl or goblet, and a silver pot to drink beer in; a silver candlestick or two, with both white lights and yellow lights of three sizes of wax; and a staff torch; a fine manchet, and a cheat loaf of bread. Thus was every chamber furnished throughout the house, and yet the two cupboards in the two banqueting chambers were not even touched. Then being past midnight, as time served they were conveyed to their lodgings to take their rest for that night. In the morning of the next day . . . they rose and heard mass and dined with my lord, and so departed towards Windsor. There they hunted, delighting much in the castle and college and in the Order of the Garter. They being departed from Hampton Court, my lord returned again to Westminster, because it was in the midst of term."

It is clear that Wolsey, however uncertain his position, was still very busy with state affairs. With Cardinal Campeggio he sat in judgement at Blackfriars over the projected divorce of Queen Catherine. Then, while his reception for the French was his last great show of hospitality there, in June 1528 he received at Hampton Court the ambassadors from Margaret of Savoy, ruler of The Netherlands, and the joining of that country with the Anglo-French alliance was confirmed in the Chapel Royal. This was known as the Truce of Hampton Court.

Wolsey's last visit to the Palace was in 1529. He had come there to escape from the very virulent "sweating sickness", sometimes known as the "English Sweat" because it was said only to attack Englishmen. "One has a little pain in the head and heart; suddenly a sweat begins and whether you wrap yourself up much or little, in four hours, sometimes in two or three, you are despatched without languishing." It was not always fatal; Wolsey suffered from it at least four times, which says much for his constitution. He feared it greatly however, and this time went into semi-retirement only allowing very few people to approach him (and those out of doors). He wrote to the King from Hampton Court to tell him of the death of Sir William Compton from this disease. Then he continued, "Sir, I cannot expresse, how hevy and peynfull it is to me to be thus farre from your grace in this casual [uncertain] and ineysy tyme, but necessitie has dryven me therunto."

37

From the middle 1520s Henry VIII was taking more and more of the government of the country on himself. Although he sent Wolsey turquoise and ruby rings as tokens of his goodwill, and he swore "I would not lose him for £20,000", he found he could now dispense with his services. Wolsey had many enemies, particularly Anne Boleyn and the Duke of Norfolk. He was accused of "praemunire" (asserting papal jurisdiction over the authority of his own country – which as legate *a latere* he was almost bound to do) and of "provision" (offering or appropriating benefices prematurely, before they had become vacant). The indictments being proved, Wolsey expected to be taken to the Tower. But perhaps because he did not defend himself, the penalty was less; he was deprived of many of his offices – no longer Lord Chamberlain nor papal legate – and much of his property, York Place was surrendered to the King (Hampton Court he already officially had) and Wolsey was sent in compulsory retirement to Esher. There he was no longer allowed his lavish furnishings nor his sumptuous way of life. He was obliged to dismiss many of his servants, and sent his jester to Henry:" If you would at this my request present the King with this poor Fool, I trust His Highness would accept him well. Surely for a nobleman's pleasure he is worth a thousand pounds." At Christmas Wolsey fell dangerously ill; the King sent his own doctor to him, and Anne Boleyn, in order to please Henry, presented him with the tablet of gold she kept hanging from her waist.

Wolsey recovered, but complained that Esher had "waxed unsavoury" (presumably due to the lack of sanitary provision). The King promptly dismantled the new gallery Wolsey had erected at Esher and set it up at Westminster, then he allowed him to move to Richmond. The Council wanted Wolsey to be further away, where he could no longer easily be in touch with the King, and recommended that he be sent to York. "Should he go not away shortly", declared the Duke of Norfolk, "I will tear him with my teeth." Wolsey replied that he would go if he were given sufficient funds, and the King granted him a thousand marks from the revenues of the Bishopric of Winchester. Accordingly he began his progress to York, where he was still Archbishop.

He travelled in considerable state and "lacked no good cheer of costly viands, both of wine and other goodly entertainment." Having arrived in York, he was greeted with much enthusiasm, and resumed his sumptuous way of life. It was planned that he should be ceremonially installed as Archbishop, for this was the first time he had been in the diocese.

Wolsey's downfall was said to be presaged by an event at Cawood Castle. He was at dinner and his great silver cross had been set up at the end of the table. A Venetian doctor, Agostino, knocked it over with his stiff black velvet gown. The cross fell on to the head of a Dr Bonner and drew blood. Wolsey rose from the table in distress, and went off to say his prayers, declaring that this was a very bad omen. So it seems to have proved. Wind might have reached London of the lordly way in which Wolsey was living, and it was feared that he might be in league with foreign powers. Henry Percy, once Anne Boleyn's suitor and now Earl of Northumberland, was sent to Cawood to arrest him for high treason. With five attendants (including the faithful Cavendish) Wolsey was conducted south towards London where he was to be tried. At Sheffield Park he was hospitably treated by the Earl of Shrewsbury; but there came Sir William Kingston, the Constable of the Tower, with twenty-four guardsmen to escort Wolsey to the King. Wolsey suddenly fell ill (he had been eating baked pears, but whether this was anything to do with it is uncertain). They paused a day, then nevertheless rode south via Nottingham to Leicester Abbey. "Father Abbot," said Wolsey, "I am come hither to leave my bones among you." After eight days' illness he died. Among his last words were said to be these:
"If I had served God as diligently as I have done the King, He would not have given me over in my grey hairs."

CHAPTER FOUR

Henry VIII's Palace

"It was never merry in England whilst we had cardinals among us."

Duke of Suffolk

Wolsey's body was buried very early the following morning.* By six o'clock the ceremonies were concluded, and immediately Cavendish and Kingston rode to Hampton Court to tell the King of the Cardinal's death. The King was in the Palace with Anne Boleyn and when Cavendish when to seek him out he found him practising his archery in the park. Feeling it more politic not to disturb him until he had finished, Cavendish leant against a tree, "intending to stand there and to attend his gràcious pleasure". The King came up behind him and slapped him on the shoulder. The surprised Cavendish went down on his knee, but the King would not let him speak, "'I will,' quoth he, 'make an end of my game, and then I will talk with you.'" It was not until evening that the King, arrayed in a nightgown of russet velvet furred with sables, finally let Cavendish deliver his news. He received it calmly and merely enquired what had become of the fifteen hundred pounds owed by the Cardinal at the time of his death.

Afterwards Cavendish had to appear before the Council, and was questioned very closely concerning Wolsey's last words. It seems that he and Kingston (who had also been interrogated) knew something it was in their interests to hide. Kingston forewarned Cavendish before he went in, "for God's sake, take good heed what you say . . . And if you tell them the truth . . . what he said, you shall undo yourself." So Cavendish protested that neither he nor Kingston had heard what the Cardinal's last words actually were. Nor did he commit them to paper when he came to write the biography. Therefore the mystery of his death has never been resolved.

* But not in the tomb he had ordered to be designed for him by Benedetto of Florence: this was eventually used to house Nelson's bones, in St Paul's Cathedral.

Henry VIII attributed to Joos van Cleve.
Showing Henry in his middle years, the painting was given to Charles I by the Earl of Arundel
in 1624.

Henry VIII's arms supported by the Lion of England and the Dragon of Wales: a 19th-century replica in Base Court.

It will be noted that the King had already installed himself at the Palace when he heard of Wolsey's death. Catherine of Aragon, still queen, was there too, following him around and showering him with compliments in the courtly Spanish fashion, to which he replied (publicly) with equal politeness. Her rooms seem to have been on the second floor, the King's on the first, and Princess Mary's at ground level. But even as early as 1528, Henry was ordering his workmen to construct lodgings for Anne Boleyn at Hampton Court. He also had them painting and refurbishing the rest of the building, and making new apartments for himself, including a new gallery, a study and a library.

In 1531 Henry put his tenure of the Palace on a more legal footing by negotiating with Sir William Weston, Prior of the Knights Hospitallers of St John. It was arranged that the King should have the Manor of Hampton Court in exchange for other properties granted to the Knights Hospitallers.

It is extraordinary that Henry left Wolsey's coat-of-arms over

42

what is now known as Anne Boleyn's Gateway, for elsewhere his men were employed in dismantling them and putting the new owner's badges in their place. At the cost of £34. 4s. 10d., the royal arms were carved in stone and set up on both sides of the Great Gatehouse and at the opposite end of Base Court. Accounts also mention the setting up of the "Kynges Beastes": dragons, lions, leopards, greyhounds and deer, in almost every part of the Palace.

These heraldic devices symbolize Henry's growing pride and self-assertiveness. In his youth he had been a blend of the pious, the scholarly and the athletic. He had written a book on theology (known as the King's Book) had allied himself firmly with the Pope, and when he did take a hand in state affairs was idealistic rather than practical. Perhaps he did not turn out to be the great patron of the Renaissance as everyone had hoped. Admittedly he did found scholarships at Oxford and Cambridge, and encouraged learning as part of a gentleman's education, yet he was to execute a fine poet in the Earl of Surrey and one of the greatest humanists in Sir Thomas More. "If my head should win him a castle in France," observed the latter, "it should not fail to go."

The King had many accomplishments: "He speaks French, English, and Latin, and a little Italian, plays well on the lute and harpsichord, sings from book at sight, draws the bow with greater strength than any man in England, and jousts marvellously."* In his twenties he was described as the handsomest prince in Christendom, he prided himself on having better legs than the King of France, and threw himself with tremendous zest into all sorts of physical activity. In the words of Giustiani,

"He is very fond of hunting, and never takes his diversion without tiring eight or ten horses which he causes to be stationed beforehand along the line of country he means to take, and when one is tired he mounts another, and before he gets home they are all exhausted. He is extremely fond of tennis, at which game it is the prettiest thing in the world to see him play, his fair skin glowing through a shirt of the finest texture."

Henry's vigour and conviviality are summed up in the words

43

---

* Pasqualigo, Venetian diplomat 1515

of his song "Pastance with good Company" (both words and music seem to be his own work).

> "Pastance [Pastime] with good company
> I love and shall until I die
> Grudge who will, but none deny,
> So god be pleased this life will I
> For my pastance,
> Hunt, sing, and dance,
> My heart is set,
> All goodly sport
> To my comfort
> Who shall me let?
>
> Youth will needs have dalliance,
> Of good or ill some pastance;
> Company me thinketh best
> All thoughts and fancies to digest,
> For idleness
> Is chief mistress
> Of vices all;
> Then who can say
> But pass the day
> Is best of all?"

For such delights Hampton Court provided the King with an ideal setting. One of his first acts on gaining possession of the Palace was to lay out nine acres of tiltyards* for jousting, which was one of his favourite sports. Spectators watched the fray from the five towers which were spaced about the field. Pavilions were set up, and the whole scene was decorated with banners, tapestries, and embroideries of gold and silver. Henry liked to take part himself, and when he did so a grand and colourful procession was formed. First came the marshal of the jousts in cloth of gold with thirty footmen to attend him, then trumpeters and drummers dressed in white damask, then forty lords many in cloth of gold, followed by twenty young knights in white velvet and cloth of silver and their pages riding on horses with trappings

44

---

* The tiltyards lie to the north-east of the Palace and are now planted as rose-gardens. One of the towers survives and is used as a restaurant.

of gold embroidery and purple. Then came the jousters who were to take part, together with their attendants, and finally the King, armed from head to foot, "with a surcoat of silver bawdakin, surrounded by some thirty gentlemen of foot, dressed in velvet and white satin, and in this order they went twice round the lists."*

Henry in his heyday never failed to acquit himself well. Giustiani describes his performance as "supernatural . . . changing his horses and making them fly rather than leap, to the delight and ecstasy of everybody."

For another of his favourite pastimes, he had the Tennis Court built in 1529–30. Royal or real tennis is an indoor game which appears to have originated in France (where it is called "Jeu de Paume") during the early Middle Ages. At first the ball was hit with the palm of the hand as this name suggests, then with a glove, and finally bats or racquets were used. The ball is solid and therefore the racquets are somewhat heavier and tougher than those used in lawn-tennis, and the ball is bounced off the walls as in squash. It is a game of great skill and has been described by a writer in *The Times* as "running, jumping and hitting chess".

Henry, of course, was adept, and the court at Hampton Court is the oldest in the country. Paving tiles were bought from John Budd of Chislehurst at sixteen shillings a thousand, masons and carpenters were employed, twelve glass windows were ordered to light the court from above, and a certain John Wylkynson paid "for 200 red ocker for pensyllyng of the new tennys play at 20*d*. the 100." The balls were put into play by servants (hence the term "service"), and the accounts include an item of five shillings paid on 16th December 1531 to "one that served on the King's side at tennes at Hampton Court".

As the King grew stouter he was no longer so quick on his feet, and it was gambling on the tennis rather than playing it which became important to him.

He staked four angels a game, but was almost invariably beaten by a young groom of the chamber called Francis Weston. Weston was one of those implicated in the accusations of adultery which

45

One of the King's Beasts on Moat Bridge: the Dragon of Wales.

were made against Anne Boleyn; and when he was executed for this reason, among his debts was a sum owing to Mistress Hannesley, wife of the keeper of the tennis courts, for tennis-balls she had provided. The balls were always expensive, being made by hand of webbing wound tightly round a core and covered in woollen cloth.

A game referred to as "open tennis play" was also played at Hampton Court – presumably a forerunner of the modern lawn tennis – and there were three bowling alleys, two indoor and one outdoor. Gambling took place here also, and inside the Palace were played all manner of games of chance – dominoes, cards, dice, shovelboard and backgammon. Gambling fever was rife; Anne Boleyn might have preferred to have played for higher stakes but Henry only gave her five pounds for "playing money", and this was all in groats so that she would not hazard too much at a time.

When the King arrived at the Palace, he generally came up the Thames and landed at a water-gate to the south-east of the main building. A passage known as the Water Gallery led from this across the gardens. In the Pond Garden the ponds themselves were set about with heraldic beasts carved in stone and standing on pillars, and the flower-beds were edged with railings painted in the Tudor colours of white and green. East of the Pond Garden (which still exists, though no longer adorned with the King's Beasts) was a hillock known as the "Mount", and this was crowned by a three-storey building called the "Great Round Arbour". The path winding up to it was edged again with heraldic beasts, and another surmounted the leaden cupola at the top of the tower. Jutting out from the main building in, it seems, a south-easterly direction, was the King's Long Gallery. In July 1534 this was added to at the further end, and the extension was floored with paving tiles, lit by twelve windows and furnished with rush mats. The room so formed was later embellished and became known as the "Riche Chamber" or "Paradise".

The flower gardens were concentrated on the south side of the Palace. Here grew roses, violets, primroses, gillyflowers and sweet williams, with borders of rosemary around the Mount.

There were also orchards of apple, pear and cherry trees and (since at that time the word did not denote plantations only of fruit trees) others such as oak, elm, holly, yew, cypress, juniper, bay, woodbine and thorn. In addition there were kitchen gardens and strawberry-plots; Princess Mary, the King's daughter, would be greeted with gifts of flowers or strawberries when she arrived at the Palace. Mostly the gardeners were paid threepence a day, but women "weding in the Kynges New Garden and at the Mount" or watering flowers received only twopence a day.

Beyond the gardens were the hunting parks. Part of these survive as Bushey and Home Parks, but in Henry's day they extended from the village of Hampton to the north-west, to Thames Ditton in the south-east. These were mainly used for the King's favourite sport of stag-hunting, but there was also a rabbit warren in Bushey Park, and the King enjoyed shooting, hawking and fishing as well, and took pride in the rearing of partridges and pheasants.

Clearly the King never had any intention of giving the Palace back to Wolsey, for he had already ordered the demolition of the old hall while the Cardinal was still alive. Also, in the autumn of 1530, foundations were laid for Henry's magnificent Great Hall, 118 feet long and 92 feet high, which still survives. The hall was completed in only four years; the King was in a hurry and had the men employed by night as well as by day, working by the light of tallow candles. Bricks were mainly brought from Hertfordshire, though there was a small brick-kiln in the park, stone mainly from Reigate, though a certain amount was shipped from Caen, and timber (mostly oak) sent from the Surrey woods. Also supplied were lead, plaster, iron and glass.

The name of Henry's architect is uncertain; it is likely that he had no architect in the modern sense. A priest called Henry Williams is described as "surveyor" with Eustace Mascall as clerk of works. The accounts for the building of the Great Hall still exist, however, and the names of the workmen are recorded. Many of them were local men from the nearby villages of Hampton, Molesey, Kingston, Chertsey and Epsom. The master mason, John Molton, was paid a shilling a day, other masons at three or four shillings a week, according to their skill and experience. The chief glory of the Great Hall is the magnificent hammerbeam roof. The master carpenter, William Clement, also received a shilling a day, the warden or overseer ninepence a day, and the other carpenters seven or eightpence a day.* A fine woodcarver from London, called Richard Rydge, made the sixteen pendant pieces that hang like lanterns from the hammerbeam, and was paid at the rate of 3s. 4d. each. He also made twenty-eight heads to be set at the foot of arches, and received a shilling each for these; another Londoner called John Hethe was paid twice as much for painting and gilding them. There is also an item,

"To John Dowsett of Kingston for 12 dosyn of tallow candylles at 18d. the dosyn spent by the carpenters working upon the vought [vault] of the Kynges new hall."

So it appears that here too the men were working overtime, even at the risk of setting fire to the whole structure.

The Great Hall was heated in the medieval way by an open fire on the floor itself, placed not quite centrally but rather nearer the top end where the King would sit. Above the fire was a wooden louvre or "femerell" – long since removed, it seems to have been a lantern-like structure, erected on the roof with the purpose of letting out some of the smoke. This, together with the rest of the hall, was decorated with stained glass designed by Galyon Hone, the King's Master Glazier.†

At the top end of the hall is an alcove, lit by a great bay-window and roofed with fan-vaulting in stone; this is where the King would sit; at the lower end a gallery for his minstrels, and below that a heavy oak screen. Outside on the battlements were twenty-nine more King's Beasts, including six great wooden lions, painted and gilded.

By 1534 the Great Hall was finished and in the following year work was begun on the Great Watching Chamber adjoining it. This was the King's guardroom, and has a fine ceiling with carved oak pendants and papier mâché insignia; coats-of-arms, the Tudor rose and portcullis and the fleur-de-lis of France (where Henry still had some possessions).

48

---

* From the accounts relating to 2nd Feb. – 1 Mar. 1533
† Galyon Hone's glass is no longer there, but some of it survives in the parish church of Earsdon, Tyne and Wear. See p. 186.

CARDINAL WOOLSEY

Cardinal Wolsey
Artist unknown

49

Astronomical Clock
This was made for Henry VIII, and dates from 1540–42. Above it hangs a bell dating from the Manor House of the Knights Hospitallers.

Great Gatehouse and Moat Bridge
The Gatehouse was built for Cardinal Wolsey and the Bridge for Henry VIII. A replica of Henry VIII's coat-of-arms was placed over the archway in Victorian times, and the set of King's Beasts was carved in 1950.

Anne Boleyn's Gateway
Seen from under the arch of the Great Gatehouse,
looking across the Tudor Base Court.

Great Watching Chamber
This was the guard-room of Henry VIII's Palace, and here his yeomen would be stationed whenever the King was in residence. The ceiling is ornamented with Tudor badges, and the walls hung with tapestries, a series of Triumphs based on the works of Petrarch – some of these almost certainly belonged to Wolsey.

(*Opposite*) The Great Hall
The Great Hall was the heart of Henry VIII's palace. The King himself would be seated on the dais at the top end of the Hall, and the whole room was warmed by an open fire on the floor (where the stone square is now). The walls are hung, as in Henry VIII's time, with tapestries depicting the Story of Abraham. Above is the magnificent hammberbeam roof, completed for the King in 1534. The stained glass by Thomas Willement is 19th century.

53

The King also turned his attention to the Chapel. There is no record that he actually rebuilt the walls, but he so transformed the interior that it is referred to in the accounts as the "Kynges New Chapell". The most important undertaking was to renew the roof. This was prefabricated; perhaps Henry did not want his chapel covered in wood shavings. The sections of the wooden vault were carved at Sonning, near Reading, on the River Thames – where timber was plentiful and of high quality – and ten or eleven woodcarvers, as well as carpenters and labourers (about a hundred men in all) worked on it there for about nine months. Careful measurements were made to ensure that the roof would fit, and when completed it was sent by section in barges to Hampton Court. In 1536 it was finally set up, and then painted and gilded by John Hethe, who had already worked on the Great Hall, and Henry Blankston. They were paid the princely sum of £451 for their work "gyltting and garnesshing of the vought in the Chapell, with great arches bourd, great pendaunts, wyth angells holdyng schochens wyth the Kynges armes and the Quenes, and wyth great pendantts of boyes playing wyth instruments, and large battens set with antyk of leade, gylte wyth the Kynges Wordde also gylt wyth ffyne golde. . ." The "Kynges Wordde" was the royal motto "Dieu et Mon Droit", which appears many times on the ceiling, and in every case except one, with the "N's" the wrong way round.

Then "Holyday Closets" were set up in the gallery (private pews or little chapels, one for the King and one for the Queen), choir stalls were carved, a new organ and chapel door made, and the floor paved. Meanwhile Galyon Hone had designed stained glass for the windows, including an east window sixteen feet high depicting St Anne and St Thomas.

Outside in the courtyard known as Clock Court, and above the terracotta Wolsey arms, Henry had installed the Astronomical Clock (or Great Clock) which was completed in 1540–42 and may still be seen today. It was made by his French clock-maker Nicholas Oursian, probably to designs by his Bavarian astronomer Nicholas Cratzer. Oursian was paid fourpence a day, Cratzer at the higher rate of five pounds a quarter. There are three dials

The Astronomical Clock
Made for Henry VIII by Nicholas Oursian in 1540–42. In the centre is the earth, on the large
pointer the sun, and there are three concentric dials made of copper. The clock indicates the
hour, the sign of the zodiac, the month, the day of the month, the number of days since the
year began, and towards the centre the quarters of the moon.

55

made of copper and rotating at different speeds, but only one hand. The clock shows the hour, the sign of the zodiac, the month, the day of the month, how many days it is since the year began, and the phases of the moon. It was important to know the latter since they determine the tides; the river was the best means to come to the Palace, and it was tidal all the way. Right in the centre of the clock is shown the earth, with lines of latitude and longitude, and on the single hand can be seen (rather smaller) the sun. This clock having been made before the publications of Copernicus in the sixteenth century and Galileo in the seventeenth, it is in accordance with the current general belief that the sun went round the earth, and not the earth round the sun.

In establishing so magnificent a palace, Henry obviously needed a large staff and extensive domestic quarters in order to maintain it. The building was surrounded by a moat, not so much for reasons of defence as for drainage. One of the reasons why kings and queens, Henry VIII among them, went on progresses, or at least used their residences in rotation, was the intolerable stench created by continuous habitation by hundreds of people for any time longer than a few weeks. Because of the moat, which would carry off effluent of all sorts into the Thames, Hampton Court was a healthier place than most. The moat could be crossed by various bridges; there was the one to the west that still exists by the Great Gatehouse, there was another on the south side – a stretch where the moat was apparently dry for there were pheasant houses underneath – and another to the east, between the King's and the Queen's apartments. The King's stool-room was strategically placed here, and across the moat somewhere on the south side was the "Great House of Easement", also called for some reason "The Lyons". This appears to date from Henry VIII's reign; there is a reference to it in the accounts for 1536 (February – March). The moat itself, however, may well have been dug in Wolsey's time (he was a stickler for hygiene); there were possibly wooden bridges across it originally, and Henry had them rebuilt in stone.

An enormous number of people were kept at the King's expense, the aristocracy not only being provided with meals at

Henry VIII's Wine Cellar

the King's table but being given "Bouche of Court" according to their rank. This was an allowance of bread, ale and sometimes wine and fuel. Some courtiers, however, had developed the habit of dining privately. It was complained in the ordinances of Eltham drawn up in 1526 for the regulation of the royal household that "sundry gentlemen noblemen and others, doe much delight and use to dyne in corners and secret places". Henry did not approve of this and ordered that they were to eat publicly in the Great Hall. It was also laid down that they should not keep greyhounds, mastiffs or any other large dogs inside the Palace, but any such should be housed in kennels at a discreet distance. The whole palace was swept by scullions twice a day. No rascals and vagabonds, "sickly, impotent, inable and unmeet persons" were allowed to hang about the Court and no dishes of stale food were to be left standing around.

The King himself did not always eat in the Great Hall, but might dine in his privy chamber "without repair of any great multitude". Only fifteen careful and trusted people served him

57

The Great Kitchen.
Built for Henry VIII. The main
fireplace in the centre is 17 feet
wide.

there: his cousin Henry Courtenay, Marquess of Exeter, six
gentlemen-in-waiting and two gentlemen ushers, together with
four grooms, a barber and a page.

Rules were laid down governing the kitchen staff; they were
to be clothed in the white and green Tudor livery, and even the
scullions were to be properly clothed. Wolsey's kitchen was
forty-eight feet long, but this was not considered adequate by
Henry, who had another, larger kitchen built alongside it. In
addition, a separate kitchen was built to cook fish in, and there
were all manner of subsidiary rooms – such as the pantry, buttery, spicery, poultry, the "squillery" where the dishes were

kept, the scalding-, boiling- and washing-houses – built round little courtyards mainly on the north side of the Palace. There were also cellars for wine. The main kitchens were placed conveniently near the Great Hall. Hatches led through to the Serving Place, then one flight of stairs to the Horn Room, where dishes could be given last minute finishing touches before being presented to the assembled company.

Such a great household could not be maintained without considerable expense, and the bills for rebuilding amounted on occasion to £400 a week. Moreover Hampton Court was not the only palace on which such expenditure was lavished. Thomas Cromwell, who succeeded Wolsey as Lord Chancellor, was most concerned at this extravagance. "What a great charge", he wrote, "it is to the King to continue his buildings in so many places at once. How proud and false the workmen be; and if the King would spare for one year how profitable it would be to him."

CHAPTER FIVE

Henry VIII: The First Three Queens

*"Squire Henry means to be God
and do as he pleases."*
                Martin Luther

Anne Boleyn, dark-haired, slant-eyed and vivacious, had captivated the heart of the King; perhaps all the more when she was unobtainable and had the attraction of forbidden fruit. Henry lavished presents on his "entirely beloved sweetheart", furs, velvets, satin and cloth of gold, and a fabulous black satin "nightgown" (or dressing-gown) lined with black fur. Not only this, but the crown jewels were sent from Greenwich to her at Hampton Court.

She was referred to as "the Lady", though the common people had worse names for her – the "witch", the "whore" – for their sympathies were generally with Queen Catherine. The Court was divided; Henry's sister Mary sympathized with Catherine, her husband Suffolk with Henry and Anne; the Duchess of Norfolk was for Catherine, her husband on the other side; Stephen Gardiner and Edmund Bonner supported the divorce, Sir Thomas More, John Fisher, the scholarly William Tyndale and Polydore Vergil, together with Sir Henry Guildford, Comptroller of the Royal Household, were all strongly against it. And as for the Pope, he was at his wit's end; "He has told me three times in secret", the Bishop of Tarbes confided to Francis I in March 1531, "that he would be glad if the marriage was already made, either by dispensation of the English legate or otherwise, provided it was not by his authority. . ."

Later that year the Pope secretly suggested, his agent told King Henry, that "your Majesty might be allowed two wives" but the agent was unsure "whether it would satisfy your Majesty's conscience." It might perhaps have suited the King, but would hardly have pleased Anne. She continued to reside at Hampton Court, enjoying the hunting, hawking and archery. Queen Catherine was there too, pathetically following Henry round and – in public – exchanging courtesies with him which he very politely reciprocated. Possibly he still retained some vague affection for her, and he never lost his fondness for their daughter Mary. But the fact remained, the Queen was well past the age of childbearing,* and he wanted a son. "Am I not a man like other men", he expostulated to the ambassador Chapuys. He already had an illegitimate boy, the Duke of Richmond, born to his former mistress Elizabeth Blount (it was at one time seriously suggested that he should marry his half-sister Mary, in order to solve the problem of succession!) and he was confident that Anne would be able to produce the much-desired male heir. In the end the strain of the ménage *á trois* became too great. The King and his Court had moved to Windsor in the summer of 1531; Catherine went too. But very early in the morning of 11th July Henry and Anne rode out on a secret hunting expedition and did not return. He never saw Catherine again; for the rest of her life she was shuffled from one country retreat to another and finally died, apparently of cancer of the heart, at Kimbolton.

By January 1532 Anne, growing ever more arrogant, was "lodged where the Queen used to be, and . . . accompanied by almost as many ladies as if she were Queen." In September that year she was created Marquess (not Marchioness) of Pembroke, and seems to have consented at last to being Henry's mistress. She became pregnant and was married secretly to the King the following January. She appeared with him publicly in April, following this up on 1st June with a splendid coronation. At this time the King ordered the refurbishing of a magnificent bed for use at Hampton Court Palace, "Also paid to John Hethe and Henry Blankston of London, paynters, for gyldyng and burnesshyng with ffyne gold and bysse [blue pigment], chassed, oon of the Kynges bed-stedes the wyche was inlarged wydder and leynggar, and for mendyng serten fawtes in the same . . . 33s. 4d."

61

* Catherine of Aragon's history of childbearing seems to have been as follows; 31st January 1510 a daughter, stillborn. 1st January 1511 a son who lived 6 weeks until 22nd February. September 1513 a son, who died at birth or soon after. June 1514 a son, died soon after baptism. Late 1514 a premature son stillborn. 18th February 1516 birth of daughter Mary. Probable miscarriage in August 1517. 10th November 1518 another stillborn child.

Anne was skilled with her needle, and it would be interesting to know if it was for this bed that she worked a tester which was still on view at Hampton Court during the reign of her daughter Elizabeth.

Numerous new rooms were being added to the Palace for the benefit of the new Queen – both state and private apartments, including a Long Gallery which appears to have been sited in the area now known as Lady Mornington's Garden, with the old wall of the moat used for its foundation. None of this remains, unfortunately, and the only glimpse visible today of the building undertaken for her is the Anne Boleyn Gateway. This was restored in the nineteenth century and what we see today is a replica; but there in the centre of the fan-vaulting is the Queen's badge, a falcon, and the initials A and H entwined in a lovers' knot.

Together with the King, the Queen received at Hampton Court an ambassadorial party from Lubeck. Strongly Protestant, the embassy displayed their motto *"Si Deus pro nobis, quis contra nos?"* (if God is for us who is against us?). They flattered the King, reviled the Pope and praised especially the break with the Church of Rome. Henry was delighted with them. But the truth was that his split with the Roman Catholic Church had been forced on him, and he may – considering his youthful piety – have suffered some inward qualms in 1531 when Pope Paul III issued a bull excommunicating him and all subjects remaining loyal to him. There had been much to alarm him, prophets and portents – Elizabeth Barton the epileptic "Nun of Kent" foretelling doom to his marriage with Anne, and in the sky a comet, and, so it was reported, a blue cross over the moon.

Henry was, however, undaunted, for it was vital that the hoped-for son should be born in wedlock. His disappointment was great when Anne's first baby turned out to be a daughter, and he began to show an interest in the Queen's ladies, and in particular Jane Seymour. Anne was unwise enough to flare up in anger when she found the King in her antechamber with Jane sitting on his knee. The shock of seeing them embracing, she declared, might endanger the child she was carrying – for she was again pregnant. "Be at peace, sweetheart," Henry tried to reassure her, "and all shall go well for thee." But Anne was not to be pacified and when a day or two later she saw Jane wearing a new locket, she was positive it came from the King and tried to tear it from her rival's neck. Then she fell into a fit of hysterics, and the incident may have precipitated her prematurely into labour; her second child, a boy, was born dead on 29th January 1536.* The King in his despair blamed her, "I will speak to you when you are well," he said icily. The Queen equally blamed him, and his dalliance with Jane Seymour. Henry was furious and stormed out of the room, "You shall have no more boys by me," he declared.

A charge of adultery was trumped up against her, and added to it a charge of incest with her brother; she and all those accused with her were imprisoned in the Tower. Jane meanwhile had discreetly retired, first to the Seymour's family seat of Wolf Hall in Wiltshire, and later to their riverside house in London. But as soon as the fate of her predecessor was determined she and her brother travelled to Hampton Court. The King joined them and his betrothal to Jane was announced to the Privy Council on the very day (19th May) that Anne was executed on Tower Green. The couple were married quietly at Westminster and Jane was proclaimed queen.

She was a shy, placid girl, not especially pretty. She had that long fair hair and pallor of complexion which were much admired in Tudor times, however, and is said to have looked her best in the rich clothes with which she was now provided. She behaved with a "pleasing sprightliness"; and after the stormy scenes with Anne, Henry must have welcomed with relief the even-tempered docility of his new bride.

At Hampton Court Palace the workmen were busy. Anne Boleyn had not lived to see the completion of her new rooms, and the task now was to replace all the insignia with those of the new queen. The "A's" were scratched off and "J's" superimposed. All over the Palace and in the gardens Anne Boleyn's falcon badge was replaced by the castle, phoenix, roses and hawthorn tree of Jane Seymour.† The royal beasts had to

63

* On the same day, Catherine of Aragon was buried at Kimbolton.
† Jane Seymour's insignia may clearly be seen on the ceiling of the Great Watching Chamber, Henry VIII's guardroom.

be altered too, and Anne's leopard transformed into Jane's animal, the panther, probably by a judicious removing of spots. Henry even had the East Window of the Chapel destroyed because it contained a figure of St Anne. Meanwhile Anne's daughter Elizabeth was declared illegitimate and made to share something of her late mother's disgrace. The four-year-old child demanded sharply, "How hap it was yesterday Lady Princess, and today but Lady Elizabeth?"

Jane Seymour does not seem to have stayed at Hampton Court until the work there was completed, but on 16th September 1537 she arrived at the Palace to await the birth of her child. The Queen was then twenty-eight years old. She had never been crowned; plans had been made for her coronation, but first an outbreak of plague (probably the dreaded sweating sickness) and then her pregnancy had forced its postponement. Everything was done to try and ensure the Queen's health and waiting gentlewomen were recruited to look after her. The mother of two of these "bought" her girls' places by sending Jane quails every week and presenting her with lap-dogs; but when the daughters arrived at Hampton Court the Queen disapproved of the plainness of their dress, and insisted that they should be provided with more fashionable head-dresses and pearls for their girdles. Their mother managed to collect together a hundred and twenty pearls, but these were not enough to please the Queen, who directed that although the girls might stay on at the Palace, they were not to attend the christening unless they were more elegantly dressed.

Queen Jane does not seem to have had a happy pregnancy despite the good predictions of the soothsayers and despite the indulgent attitude of her husband. "Why, darling, how happeneth it you are no merrier?" he asked her. The Queen took the opportunity of interceding for Catherine of Aragon's daughter Mary, now twenty years old. She was sent for from Hunsdon, where she had been living in semi-imprisonment, and brought once more to Court. "Some of you were desirous", said Henry, eyeing his courtiers, "that I should put this jewel to death."

"That had been great pity", rejoined the Queen, "to have lost your chiefest jewel of England.'' Not so, said the King, the chiefest jewel was the child in the Queen's womb, whom he confidently expected would be the long-awaited prince.

> "Queen Jane was in travail
> For six weeks or more,
> Till the women grew weary
> And fain would give o'er.
> 'O women! O women!
> Good wives if ye be,
> Go, send for King Henrie,
> And bring him to me'.''

The anonymous ballad goes on to describe a primitive Caesarian operation. Like most historical ballads, it is not strictly accurate. It was a long labour, two and a half days, but the child was born naturally at two o'clock in the morning of 12th October 1537. As soon as the birth of Prince Edward was made known there was rejoicing throughout the land. In London there was feasting in the streets, ale or wine flowed from the conduits, bells pealed, and a High Mass was held in St Paul's. "We all hungered after a prince so long", remarked Latimer, "that there was so much rejoicing as at the birth of John the Baptist."

The little prince was healthy, but babies were customarily baptized soon after birth, and it was arranged that the christening should take place in three days' time. Invitations were sent out – not too many for there was plague about. It was raging particularly in Croydon and no one from there was allowed to come. The service was to be held in the newly completed Chapel, and a great procession lined up at the door of the royal nursery. Eighty knights, squires and gentlemen came first, carrying white candles, next the choristers and clergy, after them walked the members of the King's Council, then various bishops and peers and the Comptroller and Treasurer of the Household. They were followed by the foreign ambassadors, the Lord Chamberlain, Thomas Cromwell the Lord Privy Seal, the Duke of Norfolk (who was to be one of the godfathers), and the Archbishop of Canterbury. Next came the Earl of Sussex and another lord, the Earl of Wiltshire and the Earl of Essex. The Lady Elizabeth had the duty of carrying the jewelled chrysom-cloth, but since this was very heavy, the little girl herself was carried by Edward Seymour. Then came the baby prince, in the arms of Lady Exeter, and together with her walked her husband and the Duke of Suffolk, followed by the Earl of Arundel and Lord William Howard, the nurse and the midwife. A richly embroidered canopy was held over the Prince's part of the procession, and immediately after walked his elder half-sister Mary, who was to be godmother. Lady Kingston carried the Princess's train and behind her came the rest of the ladies of the Court.

This procession passed through the old Council Chamber, along what is now known as the Haunted Gallery, through the Great Watching Chamber to the Great Hall, under Anne Boleyn's Gateway into Clock Court and along the passage to the door of the Chapel. A new silver-gilt font had been made for the christening. At the side, behind a screen, bowls of perfumed water and warming-pans with hot coals were provided in case the baby needed washing. The little prince was baptized by Archbishop Cranmer and the Garter-King-of-Arms proclaimed,

"God of his Almighty and infinite grace, give and grant good life and long to the right high, right excellent and noble Prince, Prince Edward, Duke of Cornwall and Earl of Chester, most dear and entirely beloved son to our most dread and gracious lord, King Henry the Eighth."

After this the procession re-assembled and made its way to the Queen's Bedchamber. Neither Henry nor Jane had attended the ceremony itself, but now their son was brought in to be blessed. Outside the minstrels played and the trumpets sounded in Base Court, while in the bedroom, as he held the baby in his arms, tears of joy ran down the King's cheeks.

It is not recorded how the Queen was feeling. Richly robed, she sat at the King's side and behaved no doubt with regal decorum. Three days later, however, she was seriously ill. Henry, who had stayed all the latter weeks of her pregnancy within reasonable distance of the Palace, decided to put off his intended hunting trip to Esher, and remained at her bedside. Jane had been stricken with puerperal fever. Her confessor was sent for and she took communion. Weak and delirious she struggled for life, finally at two in the morning of 25th October she succumbed and died.

It was said at the time that her death was caused by her eating unsuitably rich food, and by her catching cold through the negligence of those attending her. Then the legend grew up that she had died from a Caesarian operation – which cannot be true, as she survived for ten days after the birth. Her body was embalmed and lay in state for three weeks, first in the Presence Chamber and then in the Chapel; around it burned twenty-four candles and all the walls were hung with black. Dirges were sung and masses were said for the dead queen's soul. The mourners knelt around the bier all dressed in black. Then on 12th November the coffin was carried down into Clock Court, and a much sadder procession was lined up, with Princess Mary riding as chief mourner, behind a bier on which was a wax image of the Queen, crowned and dressed in gold tissue. They made their way slowly to Windsor, where the body was buried in St George's Chapel.

The King was too upset to attend. In the words of the same ballad,

> "The flower of Old England
> Was laid in cold clay,
> Whilst the royal King Henrie
> Came weeping away."

CHAPTER SIX

Henry VIII:
The Last Three Queens

"the state of princes in matters of marriage is far of worse sort than the conditions of poor men. For princes take as is brought them by others, and poor men be commonly at their own choice and liberty."

Anthony Denny, member of the Privy Chamber, 1540

The King now had a legitimate male heir, and Edward seemed healthy, but life was held precariously in the sixteenth century and there were many diseases which, despite the most careful precautions, might carry him off. Henry's illegitimate son, the Duke of Richmond, had just died; what certainty was there that Edward would survive? For this reason it was decided that the King should marry again. Moreover he was not suited temperamentally to being a widower. Admittedly he was growing corpulent, and beginning to have trouble with his leg – a varicose ulcer had developed which was to pain him for the rest of his life. But his physical desires seem to have been as strong as ever, and he was not in the least reluctant to consider the comparative merits of nine foreign ladies whose names were put forward. Henry was particularly excited by the portrait of Christina, Duchess of Milan, painted for him by Hans Holbein, who had become his court painter. This put him in very good humour – he ordered his musicians to play all day long and commissioned masques; a sure sign, it was thought by those around him, that he intended to marry again.

The sixteen-year-old duchess, however, was less enthusiastic. "If I had a head to spare," she is reported to have said," I might accept him." In the end, partly for political reasons, and partly based on Holbein's painting and on Cromwell's assurance that

The Chapel Royal
The Chapel was transformed for Henry VIII, with a superb carved roof prefabricated further up the Thames near Reading. The original altarpiece was destroyed during the Civil War, and a new altarpiece was later installed to replace it.

Detail of Chapel Roof
Showing one of the pendants with gilded music-making cherubs, also the often repeated King's motto "*Dieu et mon droit*" (God and my right).

(*Above*) Henry VIII and Family. Artist unknown
Henry sits with his hand on the shoulder of his young son (later to reign as Edward VII); on the other side is a posthumous portrait of the boy's mother, Jane Seymour. On either side of these three stand the two princesses, Mary and Elizabeth. Under the archway on the right is the King's Jester, Will Somers, and under that on the left a female jester, Jane the Fool.

(*Far left*) The King's Beasts
These heraldic animals flank either side of Moat Bridge. Visible here are the Lion of England, the Bull of Clarence and Jane Seymour's Panther.

The Dragon of Wales holding a shield which bears the royal arms at the time of Henry VIII, the Lions of England quartered with the Lilies of France.

(*Left*) Jane Seymour's Coat-of-Arms
This appears, together with Henry VIII's arms, on either side of the Chapel door at ground level. Jane was permitted to augment her family arms with quarterings from royal heraldry and – exceptionally – the Seymours retained this privilege after her death.

71

Aerial View of Hampton Court
This was taken from the south-east and shows how little the Palace and grounds have changed since the 18th century. The main differences are the building up of Molesey and Hampton and the making of a bridge over the Thames; the gardens are now less formal, only the Maze survives from the old Wilderness which was formerly all planted with hedges, glass-houses have been erected where the old Melon-ground was, and the deer have been removed from the park.

A View of Hampton Court by Leonard Knyff.
A bird's eye view painted with remarkable accuracy in the early 18th century,
it is very much like the present-day Palace.

she excelled the Duchess of Milan in beauty "as the golden sun did the silvery moon", the choice fell on Anne of Cleves.

The King was at Hampton Court in November 1539, awaiting news of her arrival in England. As soon as it came, he rode full speed to see her at Rochester before the official meeting at Greenwich. Whether Cromwell* and Holbein had deliberately misled the King by flattering the princess too much, or whether Anne (as is just possible) had gone out of her way to make herself as unattractive as she could, Henry was sadly disappointed.

"If I had known as much before as I know now," he expostulated, "she should never have come into this realm." Reluctantly he married her, and almost immediately set about finding grounds for an annulment. There was little problem; the marriage was not apparently consummated, and Anne seems to have been only too glad to be free of it. She spent some days at Hampton Court waiting for the formalities to be completed, and on 9th July 1540 the annulment was pronounced. Anne was granted property (including a house in Richmond), a pension of £500 a year, and a position inferior only to that of the two princesses. She remained on good sisterly terms with the King, and seems to have revelled in her new-found freedom, wearing every day "a new dress of some strange fashion or other, each one more wonderful than the last".

The King was not to stay single for long. Catherine Howard, daughter of Lord Edmund Howard, was a cousin of Anne Boleyn and a niece of the Duke of Norfolk. When she was nearly thirteen her mother died and she went to live at Horsham in the household of her grandmother, the Dowager Duchess of Norfolk, – a household where the young girl's upbringing was not very strictly supervised. While still a child she was led astray by Henry Mannox, who came there to teach the lute. Francis Dereham also lived at Horsham; he brought her little presents, a silk flower and the fabric for a quilted hat. He became her lover and called her "wife". The Howards were always an ambitious family. Catherine was transferred to Lambeth House and then introduced into Court where she became one of the ladies-in-waiting to Anne of Cleves. Small, plump, vivacious and undoubtedly pretty, it

* On 10th June 1540 Cromwell was arrested on charge of high treason as he sat in the Council Chamber at Westminster. Subsequently he was executed at the Tower of London.

was not long before Catherine caught the eye of the King. He called her his "rose without a thorn" and "jewel of womanhood" and, while he was still married to Anne, would come by barge to visit her, sometimes at night; or they would meet at the palace of Gardiner, Bishop of Winchester, who was encouraging the match.

As soon as the annulment of his marriage with Anne of Cleves was pronounced (9th July 1540), Henry was secretly married to Catherine at Oatlands Palace, and at Hampton Court Chapel on 8th August she made her first public appearance as queen. Then she dined with the King and sat next to the little Princess Elizabeth. Henry was delighted with his young wife and showered her with jewels and beautiful dresses. "The King is so amorous of Catherine Howard", the French ambassador Charles de Marillac wrote the following month, "that he cannot treat her well enough and caresses her more than he did the others." She brought into her suite various members of the old households at Horsham and Lambeth – possibly she was black-mailed into doing this – finally including her former lover Dereham who shortly became her private secretary.

Whether Catherine welcomed the King's caresses is not known; he was certainly kind, but it is unlikely that this corpulent man of forty-nine had much physical appeal to a girl thirty years his junior. His new marriage revived him somewhat; he took to rising early and riding for three hours before dinner, and he and Catherine set off for an extended wedding tour. They were back at Hampton Court for Christmas. Great festivities were held and the new Queen held court with the King. But Princess Mary was older than her new stepmother and refused to pay her the homage that Henry expected. Anne of Cleves, on the other hand, rode over from Richmond and went down on her hands and knees before Catherine. Gifts were exchanged and the King sat down amicably to supper with the two ladies. Among the dishes were pork pies made from a phenomenally large boar, which Francis I had sent as present. Henry retired to bed after feasting but Catherine and Anne danced far into the night.

The young Queen was thoroughly enjoying herself. Able for

the first time to dress as she pleased, she wore peaked head-dresses after the French fashion. The royal couple stayed on at Hampton Court and all was feasting and merrymaking until in February the King fell ill. First he had fever, then the ulcer on his leg closed up and surgeons had to open it and keep it drained. Henry recovered slowly and, with the pain from his leg, fell into a deep depression – regretting the execution of Cromwell, suspecting his present advisers, and disparaging his subjects in general.

For Catherine life now seemed excruciatingly dull. There were no entertainments, no masques, no music, no feasts – not even for Shrove Tuesday. Hampton Court was quiet and gloomy, an invalid's residence. Few visitors came, and those who did stayed only briefly. The Queen then began to seek some distraction, and found it by flirting (possibly not more than that) with a gentleman of the Privy Chamber called Thomas Culpeper.

When the King was well again he decided that they should go on a progress north as far as the city of York. He set off from Hampton Court together with the Queen, Princess Mary, most of his ministers and a whole troop of armed soldiers. The preparations were on such a lavish scale that Marillac observed "they seem to betoken some extraordinary triumph". The King longed hopefully for a second son, a Duke of York, and the greatest triumph would have been if the Queen were pregnant. She would no doubt have been rewarded with a coronation. But there was as yet no sign.

The procession set off and everywhere it halted there was feasting and celebration. For the first time, Henry's northern subjects had the opportunity to see their monarch. He cut an impressive, if bulky figure, and the pretty young Queen was much admired. All this time, however, her thoughts were still dwelling on Culpeper, and when the Court reached Lincoln she wrote to him,

"I heard you were sick, and never longed so much for anything as to see you. It makes my heart die to think I cannot always be in your company. . .

Yours as long as lyffe endures
Katheryn."

That letter, and the testimony of her servants, was to be the Queen's undoing.

The royal tour lasted five months, and on 30th October 1541 Henry and his entourage arrived back at Hampton Court Palace. On 1st November Henry attended mass in the Chapel Royal. He and Catherine knelt side by side in the Holyday Closet and took communion, the King thanking God for the good life he led and trusted to lead with his wife. On the next day, All Souls Day, when the King was again at prayer, he was handed a note by Archbishop Cranmer with the request that he should read it when he was alone.

Opening the letter, Henry read allegations of the Queen's dissolute youth, the details of which had been passed on to Cranmer by a certain John Lassels whose sister Mary* had been chamberer in the Duchess of Norfolk's household at Lambeth. The King could not believe it, he was sure that Catherine was being vilified by her enemies. But he was determined to get to the bottom of the matter and summoned the Council, including the Duke of Norfolk, in the middle of the night.

So far the accusations referred only to the Queen's early life, and it was soon made clear that they had a basis in truth. Catherine was imprisoned in her rooms, and the King (despite the fact that his young son was seriously ill at the same time) mounted his horse and rode away to Oatlands.

The passage outside the doors of the Chapel Royal at Hampton Court has become known as the Haunted Gallery, for the following legend has grown up about it. It is said that just before the King left the Palace he went into the Chapel to pray. Meanwhile the Queen escaped from her guards and came running down the gallery in an attempt to make a final plea for mercy. But the King, it is said, refused to see her and continued with his prayers, regardless of the commotion outside the door as Catherine was caught by the guards and dragged screaming back to her rooms. It is her ghost which, according to the legend, walks in the Haunted Gallery and shrieks in the middle of the night.

After the King had left, the Council proceeded to question the Queen more closely and arrested her on a charge of high treason.

---

* Mary Lassels may have been aggrieved at not receiving a post at Court, as other fellow-servants who knew the Queen's past had (possibly through blackmail) obtained.

At first she denied everything, but once they had gone she cried aloud through the night, with wild paroxysms of grief, until it was thought she would go mad or even die. In the morning, Cranmer came to see her, with a message from the King, saying he would pardon her if she confessed. So far there had been no charge of adultery, only of youthful indiscretions.

Dereham maintained when questioned that he and Catherine had been betrothed (though Catherine would not admit this and said that he had taken her by force); such a pre-contract would of course have nullified her marriage with the King, but was not otherwise culpable. In order to clear himself of any suspicion that his relationship with her had continued after this marriage, he alleged that Culpeper had taken his place in her affections and that she had been having an affair with him. Catherine admitted that she was fond of Culpeper and had given him presents, but emphatically denied that he had been her lover. He denied it too, though he had been heard to say that if the King were to die he would surely marry her.

So the case against Catherine was pieced together, and though never actually proved, there was enough evidence to condemn her. The King stormed and wept. The Queen's jewels were taken away from her and her servants dismissed. She was moved first to Syon House (on 14th November) where she stayed two months and finally to the Tower. "So weak she could hardly speak," reported the French ambassador, "she confessed in a few words that she merited a hundred deaths." She was executed on 13th February 1542.

Many of her relations were implicated. Her uncle, the Duke of Norfolk, disowned her and sided with her accusers, consequently retaining his office as Treasurer. For the rest, Lady Rochford was beheaded and the others imprisoned but − perhaps owing to Catherine's last plea for clemency towards them − were later released.

The King continued to use Hampton Court, and was there with his council soon after the Queen's death, and entertained the Emperor's ambassadors there the following June. For a year the King did not remarry. "He seems very old and grey since the mishap of the last Queen", the French ambassador reported to Francis I, "and will not hear of taking another. Although he is ordinarily in the company of ladies, and his ministers beg and urge him to marry again." But Henry, in order to avoid mishaps in the future, had put certain obstacles in his own path. It was decreed treasonable for any woman with a "past" to marry the King, and equally treasonable for her to fail to disclose it. Foreign brides were ruled out, because it was difficult to ascertain whether they had made any youthful indiscretions. Equally the ladies of the English Court were wary of the King's approaches; even if they had led blameless lives, suspicion could be enough to condemn them.

When Henry proposed to Catherine Parr in the spring of 1543, she is reported to have exclaimed, "It were better to be your mistress than your wife!"

Catherine Parr was nevertheless a highly respectable lady. Brought up in Westmorland, she had been married and widowed twice. Her first husband was Lord Borough, who died when she was sixteen, then she was married to Lord Latimer, who died in early 1543 when she was thirty. She was a small, cheerful woman, not particularly handsome but full of good sense and good will – someone who would mother the King's children and mother the King too on occasion. She had probably already fallen in love with Thomas Seymour, whom she was to marry after Henry's death, and they may well have had an understanding between them. However nothing had happened to impair Catherine's eligibility, and she agreed to the royal marriage.

The wedding was celebrated quietly at Hampton Court on 12th July 1543 in the Queen's Holyday Closet overlooking the Chapel Royal. Stephen Gardiner, Bishop of Winchester, officiated, and there were about twenty people present, including the Princesses Mary and Elizabeth. The couple spent their honeymoon at Hampton Court and were there again the following Christmas. At the Palace too, the King received the Viceroy of Sicily as an envoy from the Emperor Charles, and on his departure presented him with a golden and a silver-gilt dish.

The Viceroy had come to discuss with Henry the renewal of

hostilities against France, and in the spring of 1544 Henry set off from Hampton Court to lead his troops on a costly campaign leading to the capture of Boulogne. Meanwhile Queen Catherine stayed on at the Palace with her three stepchildren. She wrote dutifully to her husband to tell him how they were:

"My Lord Prince, and the rest of your Majesty's children are all, thanks be to God, in very good health; and thus, with my most humble commendations to your Majesty, I pray Almighty God have the same in his most blessed keeping. From your Majesty's honour of Hampton Court, the last day of July, the 36th year of your Majesty's most noble reign,

Your Grace's most humble loving wife and servant,

Catherine the Queen, K.P."

The Queen was a very devout and studious lady. As one of her household remarked," her rare goodness has made every day a Sunday, a thing hitherto unheard of, especially in a royal palace." The King did not altogether approve of women indulging in theological debate, and as for making every day a Sunday, he preferred a much more varied régime. When he was fit, and he was daily growing fatter and heavier, he would spend his day in the following way. Rising at 6 a.m. he would attend mass at seven, then if it was fine go out riding or practising his archery; if it was wet he might play bowls, for he was no longer agile enough for tennis. The main meal of the day was dinner at the early hour of 10 a.m. A fanfare of trumpets would sound as he and his family, together with any important guests, entered the Great Hall and took their place on the dais – this was at the top end of the Hall, next to the Great Watching Chamber or guardroom. By this time, bread, salts and basins of perfumed water had already been brought up from the kitchens and placed on the tables. The bread was removed while grace was said. The menu varied somewhat. It generally began with cold dishes; galantines, poultry, game, fish (very often fresh carp) and there might be stewed sparrows, larks or blackbirds. This course would sometimes be accompanied by salads of artichokes, cucumber and lettuce. Then there might be soup, and after that the principal dishes, all hot – roast venison, goose, capons, duck, pheasant, peacock, chickens or sturgeon, followed by game pies (usually venison). After that it was generally necessary to wash since at this time knives and spoons were the only cutlery used (forks were just being introduced in the aristocratic circles of Italy). The third course consisted of fruit dishes and tarts, blancmange, jellies, nuts, cheese, cream dishes and subtleties, washed down with a sweet wine called Hippocras.

Fortified by such a meal, Henry would attend to business until four in the afternoon, for by now he had assumed almost complete control of state affairs. Then supper would be served; on festive occasions there might be six different dishes for the first course and more than twice that for the second. Food was usually highly seasoned, necessary to disguise the taste if it was going bad, as it frequently was. During the meal the minstrels would play in the musicians' gallery at the bottom end of the Hall. Catherine Parr had her own little group of Italian viol players, who were paid eightpence a day.

After the tables had been cleared, there might be dancing, a concert, a masque, or other diversions. The King's chief singer was a certain James Hill, and the famous Thomas Tallis became one of the gentlemen of the Chapel Royal in 1541. For lighter entertainment there were Jane the Fool, Lucretia the Tumbler, and Henry's own jester, Will Somers.

Will Somers was hunchbacked, or nearly so, and went about the Palace with a monkey on his shoulder. He was more than a jester, he was a most trusted servant, the only man who could cope with the King in his rages and soothe him when he was in pain from his leg. As this was happening with increasing frequency, Somers became, during the last ten years of Henry's life, one of his most constant companions.

Henry was spending much of his time at Hampton Court. Since he could no longer get as far afield as Richmond or Windsor for his hunting, he had had, in 1540, all the nearby villages (Walton-on-Thames, East and West Molesey, Thames Ditton, Esher, Weybridge, Wisley, Hersham and Shepperton) enclosed with fences and stocked with game. This was called Hampton Court

81

Chase. Naturally the inhabitants were not much pleased, but had to endure it for the time being. During the next reign the fences were taken down and the land was allowed to revert to its normal use – but with the proviso that if any future monarch should wish to re-enclose it, he or she should be at liberty to do so.

By 1546–6 however, the King was growing too ill and corpulent to hunt much at all. A kind of sedan chair, called a "tram", covered in quilted velvet, was provided to move his great bulk from room to room. He still enjoyed music and indoor games such as shovelboard and backgammon. He sought relief from physical distress in preservative lozenges, liquorice pastilles and cinnamon comfits, and took to wearing glasses for reading.

The last great reception held at Hampton Court during his reign was in honour of the French ambassadors in 1546, but Henry left most of the entertaining to his young son Edward. Later that year he left Hampton Court for the last time, and moved to Whitehall. It was here in the early hours of Friday 28th January 1547 that, attended by Cranmer, King Henry died. He was fifty-five years and seven months old. His body was taken to Windsor and buried in the same grave as that of his favourite wife, Jane Seymour.

CHAPTER SEVEN

The Rest of the Tudors

"Now this is the most splendid and most magnificent royal palace of any that may be found in England, or, indeed, in any other kingdom."

Duke of Wirtemberg, 1592

Always a pale child, Edward was not always a sickly one. His very fair skin and hair were altogether in fashion, and much admired. "One of the prettiest children that could be seen anywhere," declared Chapuys the French ambassador. But it was not in the interests of the Roman Catholic powers that he should survive long; their hope was that the little boy should predecease his father. Therefore it began to be rumoured by their envoys that he was delicate, moribund, or even on occasion, dead – unless of course, a foreign marriage for him were under discussion, in which case he was reported to be big for his age and in excellent health.*

In his early years he seems to have been relatively robust, and every precaution was taken to keep him so. His apartments or "lodgings" at Hampton Court were on the north side of Chapel Court. They were swept twice a day, all his clothes and utensils were kept scrupulously clean, and a sizeable household was appointed to look after the prince and guard him from all possible ills. The cost of this was £6,500 for the year 1538–9. At the head was the chamberlain, Sir William Sidney; then there was the vice-chamberlain, a chief steward, a dean, a comptroller, a lady mistress, a nurse, and numerous women employed to rock the infant prince's cradle. His most intimate attendant was Sybil Penn, originally his wet nurse, but retained after the boy was weaned. Edward called her 'Mother Jack'† and she stayed on in the palace until her death in the reign of Elizabeth I. Henry had left Hampton Court after the death of his third wife, but was kept informed of the baby's progress. He "sucketh like a

83

---

* All these reports were issued by Chapuys at different times.
† There is a Holbein portrait drawing of her with this title.

child of his puissance," reported Cromwell. After a few weeks Henry returned to Hampton Court so that he was able to see his son almost every day, and on the occasions when he was prevented, Princess Mary visited him instead. Hampton Court was not considered altogether healthy during the summer months, and the little prince did not spend all the year there. When he was only seven months old Henry took him to his hunting-lodge at Royston, and spend the day dandling the baby, to the delight of all spectators who were watching through the window. Then Edward was moved to Havering-atte-Bower to join his sister Elizabeth under the care of Lady Bryane, who sent back news to the King, "My Lord Prince is in good health and merry. His Grace hath four teeth, three full out, and the fourth appearing."

During one of his stays at Hampton Court, when he was eighteen months old, Edward was brought in the arms of Sybil Penn to meet a group of German ambassadors who were there negotiating the King's marriage with Anne of Cleves. But the little prince, as yet unschooled in courtesy, refused to greet them or even look at them; he buried his face in his nurse's shoulder and for all their attempts to coax him into more proper behaviour, bawled and howled in fury.

Apart from this one lapse Edward seems to have been an amiable child. Princess Mary was especially fond of him and always brought him presents when she came to see him, sometimes quite expensive gifts such as an embroidered satin coat. Princess Elizabeth, being so much younger, had less money to spend, and nearly every Christmas she gave him the same thing – a cambric shirt that she had made herself.

When he was four years old and his father and Queen Catherine Howard had just returned to Hampton Court after their triumphant progress to the north of England, Edward suffered his first serious illness. This was what was then termed "quartan fever", a disease in which the patient's temperature soars every third or fourth day. At the same time, therefore, that his stepmother was arrested for infidelity and imprisoned in her rooms, the prince not many yards away was fighting for his life. But his strong constitution stood him in good stead and gradually he recovered. The Queen was sent to the Tower, the King departed for Oatlands, and Edward was visited by Princess Mary before being sent to convalesce at Ashridge.

This was the pattern of Edward's life during his early years: from time to time he was sent into the country because it was healthier, and from time to time he was brought to Court because his father wished to see him, and wanted him to be schooled in etiquette. When he was six years old his academic education was taken over by John Cheke, humanist and professor of Greek at Cambridge, with the recommendation from his former teacher Dr Cox that already he "understandeth and can frame well his three concords of grammar and hath made forty or fifty pretty Latins and . . . is now ready to enter into Cato and to some profitable fables of Aesop." Cheke continued this careful and thorough education, and became Edward's lifelong friend and mentor.

In 1546 there was a great reception at Hampton Court in honour of D'Annebault the Lord High Admiral of France who came accompanied by two hundred courtiers in order to finalize a peace treaty between his country and England. Henry VIII being by this time very portly and decrepit, he entrusted his eight-year-old son with greeting him when they arrived. Edward was unsure of his French, since he had only just begun to learn the language, so he wrote to ask his stepmother Catherine Parr whether she thought that the Admiral would understand Latin. On 23rd August the young prince rode from Hampton Court to meet the party at Hounslow. With him came the Archbishop of York, the earls of Huntingdon and Hertford and eight hundred gentlemen and retainers dressed in cloth of gold. Edward himself wore a jewelled doublet of crimson and white satin. They met on the riverbank, for the French party had come up the Thames from the Tower. The Prince dismounted, bowed, kissed the Admiral on both cheeks, and made a short speech of welcome – acquitting himself very well this time – before they rode back side by side to the Palace.

There Edward conducted the Admiral to his apartments, where refreshments were waiting, and presented him with gifts of gold and silver plate on behalf of his father. It was not until the next day that the Admiral saw the King. The pact between the two countries was solemnized at mass in the Chapel, and then the whole company had six days of hunting and feasting before the Frenchmen left.

When, in the following year, King Henry died, Edward was nine years old. At the time he was staying at Ashridge; but his uncle Edward Seymour (Lord Hertford) took him from there to Hunsdon, where Elizabeth was, so that brother and sister could hear the news together. They burst into tears. Edward was proclaimed king, and in February was crowned by Cranmer at Westminster.

Though crowned king, Edward was allowed very little say in state affairs, and the real power during the early years of his reign was in the hands of the same Lord Hertford, Duke of Somerset, who had told him of his father's death, and who now assumed the title of Protector. Edward constantly complained that while his uncle was using the royal plural and addressing the King of France as brother, he was not being treated like a king at all. Moreover he was kept short of pocket-money. He applied to his other uncle, Thomas, who gave him some – though he obviously expected favours in return. Thomas Seymour was ambitious; he was created Lord High Admiral, tried proposing to Princess Elizabeth but was refused, and then, with Edward's permission, married Catherine Parr. Catherine, however, died in childbirth in the autumn of 1548. Thomas Seymour, finding his status now diminished, plotted to supplant his brother, marry Edward off to his ward Lady Jane Grey (instead of Mary Queen of Scots as Somerset planned) and thus gain tremendous power. He hoped to enlist his nephew's support. He therefore went to Hampton Court, where the King was staying, and found him walking with Somerset in one of the galleries. "Since I saw you last," began Thomas, "you are grown to be a goodly gentleman, and I trust that within three or four years you shall be ruler of your own things." "Nay," the boy replied. Thomas went on to say that by the time he was sixteen Edward would be able to choose his own advisers; but the boy would not be drawn and said nothing.

Thomas concluded that he would get nothing out of the King

Edward VI
Painting attributed to Guillim
Stretes; at Hampton Court.
Showing the young king aged
13½, this was possibly a
marriage portrait.

87

unless he was able to see him alone. The best time for this would be at night he thought, so on the night of 16th January 1549 he armed himself with a pistol and, with two of his servants, entered the Palace via the Privy Gardens. From there they made their way into the apartments where Edward slept, guarded by his little dog. But Edward had got up in the night, put the dog beyond the outer door to his rooms, and then gone back to bed, bolting the inner door behind him. When the Admiral attempted to enter, the dog was alerted and barked at him furiously; whereupon the Admiral, in a panic, shot him. The whole household was aroused by the commotion, and all the explanation that Seymour could give was, "I wished to know whether His Majesty was safely guarded." He was promptly arrested, sent to the Tower and subsequently executed by order of his brother. His nephew, understandably, did not raise a finger to reprieve the uncle who had shot his pet dog.

Somerset, though astute in many ways, had never been much liked by his peers. He was too proud and ostentatious, and ordering the execution of his own brother did nothing to increase his popularity. By September 1549, in the words of Holinshed's Chronicle, "many Lords of the Realm, as well as Councillors, misliking the government of the Protector, began to withdraw themselves from Court, and resorting to London fell to secret consultation for redress of things." Warwick and the rest did not like to see so much power in the hands of this one young man. Report of this secret consultation reached Somerset, who was with Edward, Cranmer and others at Hampton Court. The Council may not have intended that Somerset should fall, only that his power should be lessened. The Protector, however, treated it as a threat and issued the following proclamation in the King's name:

"EDWARD. – The King's Majesty straightly chargeth and commandeth all his living subjects with all haste to repair to His Highness at his Majesty's Manor of Hampton Court, in most defensible array, with harness and weapons, to defend his most royal person and his entirely beloved uncle the Lord Protector, against whom certain have attempted a most dangerous conspiracy. – And this to do in all possible haste. Given at Hampton

Court the 5th day of October in the third year of his most noble reign."

In towns and villages round about handbills were posted enlisting the aid of all men to help defend the King and the Protector, suggesting that if the latter were deposed the King's life would be in danger. Another more extreme notice was put up in London attacking the "crafty traitors" who were planning "the Lord Protector's death . . . to plant again the doctrines of the Devil and Anti-Christ of Rome." A thousand men were sent to London to defend the Mayor and Corporation and the gates were closed at the Tower.

At Hampton Court the Palace was fortified, for the first and only time in its history. Five hundred men stood guard, five hundred suits of armour having been hastily gathered to equip them. The moat was filled – no doubt the pheasants were sent packing from where they had been nesting under one of the bridges – the gates defended and the battlements manned.

Meanwhile Somerset sent his son, Sir Edward Seymour, with a letter signed by the King asking Lord Russell and Lord Herbert to send reinforcements. Sir William Petre was also sent to parley with the Council, but did not return, for he had been won over by Warwick and joined the other side.

All day they waited at Hampton Court Palace. There was no sign of the hoped-for reinforcements, only a crowd of local people had collected the other side of Moat Bridge. The King, who was troubled with a cold, went to bed. Meanwhile Somerset realized that if the Palace were to be attacked and besieged, it could not hold out for long if there were no organized support from the surrounding district. So in the middle of the night he woke up Edward, and placed him in the centre of a small procession of his remaining supporters, flanked by yeomanry and preceded by trumpeters. Leaving their horses in Base Court, they walked through Wolsey's Great Gatehouse, across Moat Bridge and out among the crowd. There they stopped. The King spoke first. "Good people," he said, "I pray you be good to us – and to our uncle." The crowd cheered. Then the Protector declared, "If I am destroyed, the King will be destroyed, kingdom, commonwealth – all will be destroyed together.'' The people were silent. Somerset directed the King back into the Palace, they mounted the waiting horses and galloped back across the bridge. As they passed through the crowd the boy is said to have waved his jewelled dagger and shouted, ''Will ye help me against those who would kill me?'' and the people replied, ''God Save Your Grace! We will die for you!''

But the eleven-year-old boy had no option. He had to go where Somerset took him, which was to Windsor Castle. Full of cold and in growing fear of his uncle, Edward fretted and compared the castle unfavourably with the palace he had left, ''Methinks I am in prison,'' he confided to Paget, ''here are no galleries nor no gardens to walk in.''

A deputation was sent to mediate with the Councillors, civil war was averted, and Somerset was sent to the Tower for three months. Edward returned to Hampton Court where he celebrated his twelfth birthday, and three days after that rode in state, resplendent in cloth of gold, through the City of London.

Edward was back at Hampton Court again in the early summer of 1550, entertaining visiting young courtiers from France with jousting, bull- and bear-baiting, hunting and a good supper. The King was in great form, and the Frenchmen were impressed with his vigour and good humour.

The custom was that when the sweating sickness was rife in London, the King and his circle would retreat from town, very often to Hampton Court. This reason brought Edward there in 1551, together with his uncle Somerset, by this time at least partially restored to power.* Here they received the Marshal de St André, and two other envoys sent by the King of France to invest Edward with the Order of St Michael; this was in exchange for Henry II's being invested with the Order of the Garter and to cement the alliance between the two countries.† The French embassy arrived on the morning of 14th July; Edward received them in the Presence Chamber and addressed them in his by now excellent French. The investiture itself took place two days later. Carlois, secretary to de Vieilleville one of the ambassadors, wrote a description of the celebrations. Edward appeared, he said, ''an

---

* The Duke did not enjoy his power for long. He was plotting to overthrow the Reformation,
† It was also proposed that Edward should marry the French king's daughter Elisabeth.
was opened by Edward VII in 1909; but the Tijou screens were later restored to the Palace.

angel in human form; for it was impossible to imagine a more beautiful face and figure, set of by the brilliance of jewels and robes, and a mass of diamonds, rubies and pearls, emeralds and sapphires – they made the whole room look as if lit up." After the ceremony in the Chapel, a banquet was held in the Great Hall, followed by jousting and a concert. Feasting, hunting and tournaments continued until the 23rd of the month. During his stay the Marshal de St André attended the King's levée in his state bedchamber and was much impressed by its furnishings – Italian murals, tapestries of biblical scenes and paintings by Holbein.

In April 1552, Edward fell seriously ill with, according to the diary that he kept, smallpox and measles at the same time. It seems hardly credible that anyone could survive having both diseases at once, and it is likely that it was just a bad attack of measles. Though he recovered within a fortnight, the illness seems to have undermined his constitution, and left him, for the first time in his life, delicate. He was at Hampton Court twice more during the summer of 1552. On 27th June he received, without great enthusiasm, the Emperor's ambassador, de Scheyve, come to enlist the support of the English against the French; and Edward seems to have been there again on 29th September.

By the New Year, however, he had developed tuberculosis – it may well be that the measles had left him a prey to it – and when he emerged again into public life, everyone was shocked to see how white and thin he had become. After much suffering, aggravated rather than alleviated by the ministrations of a quack doctor, he died miserably at Greenwich on 6th July 1553, aged fifteen and three-quarter years.

During the last weeks of his life, Edward has been persuaded by the Duke of Northumberland to set down on paper the "King's Device" for the succession to the throne. In its final draft, this excluded both his half-sisters on the grounds of illegitimacy, and decreed that should he die without issue (as he knew he would), the crown should go first to the Duchess of Suffolk's sons (there were none). After that, Edward had originally written, it should go to the "Lady Jane's heirs males" – but this was altered, possibly by Northumberland, to "the Lady Jane, and her heirs males". Lady Jane Grey had just been married, much against her will, to Northumberland's son Lord Guildford Dudley. The Council had signed the King's Device, so on Edward's death Lady Jane was proclaimed Queen. Mary meanwhile, instead of attending her half-brother's deathbed, had fled to Framlingham in Suffolk. Northumberland rode in that direction at the head of a small force of troops raised by the Council in order to counter her claim to the throne; but thousands had flocked to Mary's support, so Northumberland, hearing too that the Council had had a change of heart and were now proclaiming *her* Queen, capitulated without a confrontation. He was sent to join Lady Jane and Dudley in the Tower, and Mary entered London in triumph.

For the first time (if one discounts Matilda), the country was to be ruled by a woman, but it was not accepted that she should rule alone; she must marry. One of the things her father regretted on his deathbed was that this had not yet been achieved. She had been betrothed as a child of seven to Emperor Charles V but nothing had come of that. Now there were two possible English candidates: Reginald Pole (who was not yet a Cardinal) and Edward Courtenay, Earl of Devon. Courtenay was a great-grandson of Edward IV, and though he had been in the Tower for fifteen years, this was the match recommended by the Council. Mary, however, had other ideas. She took the advice of Charles V to marry into the Hapsburg line, and arranged to wed, by proxy in the first place, Philip of Spain.

Even more unpopular than the re-establishment of the mass, and the re-forging of the links with the Church of Rome, was the idea of this Spanish marriage. Anti-Spanish feeling allied to Protestant zeal was especially strong in London and the home counties, and found expression in the Wyatt Rebellion, the intention of which was to depose Mary and set up Elizabeth as queen, marrying her this time to that eligible bachelor Courtenay. The rebellion failed, but London was still likely to be the scene of anti-Spanish demonstrations. Therefore when, in July 1554 five months after the proxy marriage, Philip had landed at Southampton, the actual marriage was celebrated at Winchester. By the terms of the contract, Philip was declared king (though he was never crowned) but Mary was to have supreme authority, and should she die childless Philip's kingship should end immediately.

Then, on 19th August, the couple entered London and processed through the city with great pageantry. They did not stay long, for there was always some undercurrent of insurrection in the capital, and it must have been with some relief that on 23rd August they retired to Hampton Court for their honeymoon. It would be a mistake, however, to regard this day as one of unmitigated bliss. Philip behaved most courteously and was always at the Queen's side, but he was sadly disappointed in his bride who, at thirty-eight, was considerably older than he and not particularly attractive. "Ugly, small, lean, with a pink and white complexion, no eyebrows, very pious and very badly dressed": that is how one of his followers described her.

The couple shut themselves away, there was no feasting as there would have been in her father's day. They dined behind closed doors on fish, buttered eggs and oatmeal, leaving the Spanish attendants to quarrel with the English, and the English with the Spanish. Philip's gentlemen found fault with the ladies of the Court, called them dowdy, uncouth and lacking in grace; while they, it was admitted, "care equally little for the Spaniards. The English in fact, hate us as they do the devil . . . They cheat us in the town, and anyone venturing in the country is robbed."

Whatever his feelings for her, Mary was passionately in love with Philip, and came to believe that she was going to bear his child. She announced this in November 1554, and must have appeared to be pregnant, for few people doubted it. "Long persuasion had been in England", wrote Foxe in his *Book of Martyrs*, "with great expectation, for the space of half a year or more, that the queen was conceived with child. This report was made by the queen's physicians, and others nigh about the court; so divers were punished for saying the contrary and commands were given that in all churches supplication and prayer should be made for the queen's good delivery . . ."

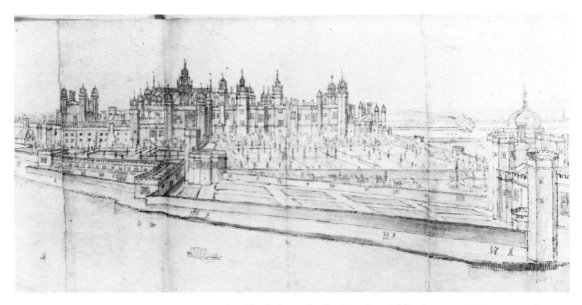

Hampton Court Palace
A section from a panoramic view of London drawn by Antonis Wyngaerde. This shows the appearance of the Palace in the time of Mary I, after it had been largely rebuilt by her father Henry VIII. To the left is Wolsey's Gatehouse, then the Great Hall with its 'femerell' is silhouetted against the sky-line, then the numerous turrets surmounting the old Cloister Green. The onion-shaped roof presumably covers the room called 'Paradise', and on the extreme right is the Water Gallery where Mary Tudor held her half-sister Elizabeth prisoner.

It was decided that the baby should be born at Hampton Court. The custom for a royal birth was for the queen to shut herself away for a month before the baby was due. Mary and Philip came to the Palace on 3rd April 1555 to celebrate Easter and await the expected confinement.

Childbirth was a hazardous ordeal, and especially so for a woman expecting her first child at the age of forty. There was thought to be a strong possibility that the Queen would not survive. In this event, Philip had been excluded from the succession (though he was empowered to act as regent should Mary have a child that lived), and the real choice was between Elizabeth and Mary Queen of Scots. Since Mary Queen of Scots was firmly allied to the French and had no sympathy with the Spanish, it was thought – especially by Philip – marginally preferable that Elizabeth should succeed. Therefore Elizabeth was brought from Woodstock, where she had been residing under virtual house-arrest, to Hampton Court. But to her chagrin, instead of being welcomed on more or less equal terms by her half-sister, she found herself imprisoned in the Water Gallery.* Having been already once imprisoned in the Tower, and not knowing what were the Queen's intentions towards her now, she went in fear of her life.

Just before Elizabeth arrived there was held a St George's Day procession around the courts and cloisters of the Palace – Philip in his Garter robes, the Lord Chancellor and members of the Council, Bishop Gardiner, lords, knights and churchmen, with trumpets sounding and the choir singing *"Salve Festa Dies"* (Hail, Blessed Day). The Queen did not participate, but in order to dispel the rumour circulating that she was dead, she looked out of her bedroom window as they passed through Cloister Green.

Meanwhile all the preparations were made for the expected birth; midwives and nurses were engaged and women to rock the cradle. Letters were drawn up to announce the fact to all the Christian world. They were signed by Mary and Philip, only the date was left blank, and on most of them the sex of the child was undetermined using the French "fil-" to which an "s" could be added if it were a boy, or "le" if it were a girl. But to Cardinal Pole, Mary confidently announced "the gladding of us with the happy deliverie of a prince".

Although a notice had been pinned to the door of the Palace, "Shall we be such fools, good Englishmen, to believe that our Queen is with child", by the end of the month Mary was said to be actually in labour. Bells were rung, toasts drunk, thanksgivings said and bonfires lit. Yet nothing happened.

The Queen was sure, however, that within a few days the baby would be born. She sent her husband to visit Elizabeth, still imprisoned in the Water Gallery. What passed between them is unknown, but the Princess was kept in solitary seclusion for another two weeks. Then Elizabeth was interviewed by Gardiner and certain lords; and while not admitting any guilt of conspiring against the throne, she was careful not to express any resentment. "It were much better", she assured them, "to me to lie in prison for the truth, than to be at liberty, suspected by my Prince."

After a further week, Elizabeth was summoned to appear before the Queen. Full of trepidation, she was escorted across the garden to the Queen's lodgings, and then ascended alone to the royal bedchamber. There she found her half-sister enthroned

95

---

* This lay to the east of the William II Banqueting House that exists today.

in state. Once more she was interrogated, with Philip quite possibly listening behind the arras. If she had, as she maintained, done nothing wrong, did she consider herself to have been wrongfully imprisoned? But Elizabeth was not to be caught in this trap. "I cannot and must not say so to your Majesty," she replied. Did she then complain to others, demanded the Queen. No, said the girl, she kept her troubles to herself. The Queen deliberated. "God knows," she muttered, and finally pronounced her forgiveness. Another week and Elizabeth was liberated and allowed to live once more in a style appropriate to a princess.

Meanwhile there was still no baby. Mary was suffering from pseudocyesis (phantom pregnancy). Swollen-bodied, haggard-faced, she shut herself away week after week, lying miserably in bed or (according to a French spy who had the information from one of the midwives) sitting hunched on the floor with her chin on her knees, vainly willing this impossible birth.

On 11th June, according to Foxe's *Book of Martyrs*, a London woman called Isobel Malt had just given birth to a son at her home in Aldersgate when she was approached by Lord North and another lord and asked whether she would "part with her child, and would swear that she ne'er knew nor had such a child." They are said to have attempted to bribe her "with many fair offers". But, the story goes, she would not give up her son, and Timothy Malt grew up in obscurity.

There survives to this day at Hever Castle in Kent a set of baby clothes delicately stitched in white silk, made by the Princess Elizabeth for the child her half-sister never bore.

In order to save the Queen's face somewhat, and to put an end to the constant rumours and ribald remarks, processions and "*Te Deums*", the Court moved on 3rd August 1555 for a short visit to Oatlands. Philip, tiring of his barren wife and the anti-Spanish feeling fostered by almost everyone but her, went back to Spain, not returning until nineteen months later. He came briefly to Hampton Court in order to hunt. However, by that time Mary, prematurely aged and depressed to the point of madness, was sinking slowly to the grave. Early in 1558 she fondly imagined herself pregnant again – another delusion – and she died on 17th November, leaving in her will certain jewellery to her husband "to dispose of at his pleasure, and, if his highness think meet, to the issue between us".

Elizabeth had left Hampton Court very discreetly, as soon as it was clear that her half-sister's pregnancy was a myth. Then she rejoined the Queen at Greenwich, evaded suspicion of rebellion, lay low at Hatfield, wrote diplomatic letters, and finally on 6th November 1558 she was recognized (reluctantly) by Mary as her successor. Mary expressed the hope, vain as the rest of her hopes, that her sister would preserve the Roman Catholic religion.

Elizabeth was hardly likely in the long run to lend whole-hearted support to a faith which denounced her as illegitimate and her claim to the throne consequently spurious. She was at Hatfield when she was told of her accession to the throne, and she was crowned amidst great celebration on 15th January 1559. Loyalty to the new queen was immediate, unhesitating and almost universal. "There is not a heretic or traitor in the country" sourly remarked one of Philip's adherents, "who has not started as if from the grave with expressions of great pleasure."

It was customary for the Court to move from palace to palace according to the season, and according to the prevalence of plague – and to the conditions of sanitation. Elizabeth's famous progresses, when she travelled around the country with her whole entourage and more than three hundred baggage carts, were partly on this account, partly for reasons of economy, and partly so that her face should become known to a great many of her subjects. Her first visit as queen to Hampton Court began on 10th August in the summer after her accession, when she came there from Nonesuch in Surrey. She regarded the Palace primarily as a place of recreation, and it was here too that she would entertain her various suitors.

In the early part of her reign, few people doubted that Elizabeth would marry, and she had a great many suitors both from this country and abroad. One of the first was the Earl of Arran, a Protestant member of the royal house of Scotland.* He had managed to escape from France, and came secretly to

97

---

* If she had married him the unification of England and Scotland would have happened nearly fifty years earlier, instead of having to wait until her death.

Hampton Court so that the Queen might meet him. He crossed the river from the Surrey side, and the trusty Cecil, Lord Burghley, who had been made principal secretary to Queen Elizabeth within three days of her accession, met him on the bank and took him to see her in the Privy Garden. She was not impressed. However suitable the match might have been politically, she found him slow-witted, apathetic, not even handsome, and lacking all the virility she liked to see in a man. So the idea was dismissed summarily and and a few days later when the French ambassador asked if she would have the refugee arrested if he should ever turn up in England, she agreed without hesitation.

Ambassadors from other suitors came to see her at Hampton Court – from Philip of Spain who, having failed to wed her himself, now proposed his cousin the Archduke Charles, and from the King of Sweden on behalf of his son Prince Eric. The Archduke she might have considered seriously if he had agreed to sail to this country to meet her, which he never did; and as for Prince Eric, his suit was literally laughed out of Court.

The only man Elizabeth really seems to have loved, and genuinely thought of marrying, was Robert Dudley, later Earl of Leicester. Elizabeth later denied that their relationship had ever been anything but platonic, yet in the spring of 1561 she had him moved from the ground-floor rooms he was already occupying at Hampton Court to accommodation next to her own. Rumour was that they were living together as man and wife, and it may well be that she was not quite the virgin queen that she liked to be thought. Years later, a young man turned up in Madrid claiming to be the son of Elizabeth and Leicester. His story was that in the autumn of 1561 Kate Ashley (one of the Queen's most faithful attendants) had summoned her servant Robert Sotherton to the Palace, where he was told that a noble lady had just given birth. He was asked if he would have the boy christened Arthur, and bring him up as his own son. He smuggled the baby out of the Palace and gave it to the miller's wife at Molesey to nurse; then later he had the boy brought to his own house, and he sent him to school in London. When he grew up Arthur travelled abroad, and only learnt his true iden-

Elizabeth I
Artist unknown. The portrait shows the Queen's appearance in the early 1580s.

tity when his adoptive father was on his deathbed. The story is circumstantial and reasonably credible.

Whether or not she gave birth in the autumn of 1561, a year later Elizabeth was in the Palace desperately ill. She had arrived on 19th September. At first she seemed in perfect health, and spent some weeks alternating attending to state affairs with indulging the love of music she had inherited from her father. (She was quite an accomplished performer on the lute and the virginals.) She first began to feel ill on 13th October. Impatient with any sort of indisposition, she took a bath and went for a walk in the Palace gardens. That evening she developed a high temperature, and within two days her condition was critical. The Queen had smallpox. Cecil was sent for and the Council alerted, for Elizabeth was in a near-coma and the doctors were convinced she had not long to live. In this belief, the lords urgently debated the question of succession. The name of the Earl of Huntingdon was put forward, so was that of Catherine Grey, sister of the unfortunate Jane – oddly enough there was little support for the Queen's young cousin, Mary Queen of Scots. Elizabeth herself, weak and delirious, entreated the Council to make her beloved Robert Dudley Protector of England, with a title and twenty thousand pounds a year.

Then the rash developed, the crisis passed, and with amazing rapidity the Queen recovered. She had Dudley made a Privy Councillor, also the Duke of Norfolk, so that he should not be jealous.*

Elizabeth was not the only one to be struck down with smallpox at this time. Sybil Penn, Edward VI's old nurse, who had been allowed to stay on in apartments at Hampton Court, also caught it. She died on 6th November, and was buried in Hampton Church. But it seems that her tomb had been desecrated even before the church was rebuilt in 1829, and there are persistent rumours that her ghost (sometimes appearing as a woman working at her spinning wheel) still haunts the Palace.

It was at Hampton Court that the Queen was visited in 1564 by Melville as envoy for Mary Queen of Scots. Elizabeth had suggested, astonishingly, that Mary should marry Robert

---

* There was a certain animosity between the two. The Queen was watching them play tennis when, growing hot, Dudley snatched her handkerchief and wiped his face with it. Norfolk, furious, threatened to hit him in the face with his tennis racquet, at which the Queen was "offended sore with Dudley".

Dudley, and had him created Baron of Denbigh and Earl of Leicester. Elizabeth had never met her cousin, and was curious to know how they compared in looks and accomplishments. Who was the fairer, she or Mary? Melville replied that she was the fairest in the English court and Mary in the Scottish. Then she continued, which of them was the taller? On being told Mary was, Elizabeth said that in that case she was *too* tall. Then she asked about the Scottish queen's accomplishments – did she play well on the lute and the virginals? Melville was forced to admit that although she performed "reasonably for a Queen", she did not have Elizabeth's proficiency, nor did she dance "so high and disposedly".

For her part, though Elizabeth was to be courted almost all her life, the discussions often taking place at Hampton Court, negotiations invariably fell through. For if she married a foreign prince, there was a danger that England would be subjected to his country, and if it were an Englishman he would be invested with an unprecedented degree of power. Whereas if she stayed unmarried yet marriageable, her authority was unchallenged. Her passion for Robert Dudley she largely kept in check, although he danced attendance on her for years, and although she treasured his picture and his letters.

Foreign visitors to Hampton Court found it an enchanting place. Paul Hentzner from Germany wrote about the Palace in his *Travels in England* (1598). The Audience Chamber he described as adorned with "tapestry of gold, silver and silk of different colours; under a canopy of state are these words embroidered in pearl: *VIVAT REX HENRICUS OCTAVUS*. Here is besides a small chapel richly hung with tapestry, where the Queen performs her devotions. In her bedchamber, the bed was covered with very costly coverlids of silk . . ." In the Great Hall, apart from the portraits and tapestries he noted the following: "curiosities: a very clear looking-glass, ornamented with columns and little images of alabaster; . . . an artificial sphere; several musical instruments . . . the bed in which Edward VI is said to have been born, and where his mother Jane Seymour died in childbed . . . numbers of cushions ornamented with gold and silver; many counterpanes and coverlids of beds lined with ermine; in short, all the walls of the Palace shine with gold and silver. Here is also a certain cabinet [room] called Paradise where besides that everthing glitters so with silver, gold and jewels, as to dazzle one's eyes, there is a musical instrument made all of glass except the strings."

The 'Paradise' or 'Riche Chamber' was situated at the end of the King's Long Gallery. It was painted white, gold and black, and ornamented with a gold and blue crown and a rose, (a golden rose was Elizabeth's device). The roof too was painted and gilded, and the room was full of rich tapestries and royal robes. It was also said to contain "a beautiful large unicorn's horn".

As well as enriching this particular room, Elizabeth had built at the Palace new stables, and an ingenious fountain in what is now Clock Court. This was made in black and white marble and was surmounted by a figure of Justice. The Duke of Wirtemberg described it as "a splendid, high and massy fountain, with a waterwork, by which you can if you like make the water play upon the ladies and others who are standing by, and give them a thorough wetting."

When she was at Hampton Court in September 1572, Elizabeth fell ill again, allegedly a second attack of smallpox. Leicester sat up all night at her bedside, and she recovered remarkably quickly. She was back again at the Palace before the end of the year, to keep Christmas there.

Christmas at Hampton Court became a custom with her, and often she would stay on two months into the new year. She liked to celebrate it with great festivity. The Great Hall was illuminated with oil lamps strung across on wires, and the banquets were alternated with dancing, masques and plays. In 1576 the latter included "The Historie of Error showen at Hampton Court on New Year's Day at night, enacted by the children of Powles" (*The Comedy of Errors*?), and on Twelfth Night a play about Mucius Scaevola. Expensive gifts were always exchanged at this season; those which Elizabeth herself gave generally being far exceeded in value by those her courtiers gave her. They strove to outdo each other; some gave gold coins, some gave dresses or jewellery. In 1576 the Countess of Derby presented the Queen with a beautiful embroidered white satin petticoat, Cecil thirty pounds in a purse, and the Earl of Leicester "a carcanet of gold, enamelled garnished with sparks of diamonds and rubies, and pendants of pearls."*

While the Court, having held Christmas there, was still in the Palace in February 1594, there was a robbery. Four gentlemen (Bryan Annesley, Francis Hervey, James Crofts and John Parker), who were lodged in one of the tiltyard towers, came back on the evening of the 2nd to find that their rooms and trunks had been broken into, and money and jewellery to the value of £400 had been stolen. The crime was traced to a certain John Randall, who was accused and hanged.

This was a minor matter, however, compared with a plot on the Queen's life. She had a physician called Dr Lopez, a Portuguese Jew. He was suspected by Robert Devereux, Earl of Essex, (Elizabeth's favourite at this time) of attempting to murder her by mixing poison with her medicine. "I have discovered a most dangerous and desperate treason," wrote Essex to Anthony Bacon in January 1594. He, Burghley and Cecil were instructed to investigate the matter, and to begin with could find no firm evidence to support the accusation. Elizabeth was furious with Essex and summoned him to her privy chamber at Hampton Court; he was a "rash and temarious youth", she declared, "to enter into a matter against the poor man which he could not prove." Essex, equally angry, stormed out, and sulked for two or three days in his rooms with the door shut. In the end Elizabeth decided to forgive him. The matter of Dr Lopez was looked into further, and it was discovered that Philip II had offered him a considerable bribe if he would murder the Queen. Whether he was going to accept the bribe or not was never really proved, but Lopez was tried and condemned.

Elizabeth had always loved Hampton Court. She was particularly fond of the gardens, where she used to go for a brisk walk before breakfast. The gardens were well maintained in her reign, and full of very carefully trained plants, not only flowers but herbs – there were walls completely covered with rosemary. She

* Nichol's *Progresses of Queen Elizabeth*

had pleasant arbours set up here and there in the gardens, and also sometimes in the Park, where she went hunting, "a delicate bower being prepared, under the which were her Highness's musicians placed, and a cross-bow by a nymph, with a sweet song, delivered to her hands to shoot at the deer." For the Queen loved pageantry as well as sport.

Elizabeth's last known visit to the Palace was in September 1599, when despite the fact she was in her sixties, she was seen through a window dancing merrily to a pipe and tabour. She left Hampton Court a few days later, on horseback even though the weather was very bad. She was furious when Lord Hunsdon remarked, "It was not meet for one of her Majesty's years to ride in such a storm." "My years!" she thundered, "Maids, to your horses quickly!"

It was characteristic of her to resent anyone commenting on her age or remarking that she was in any way less strong or beautiful than she had been in her youth. Even when she was dying she refused to go to bed, but sat propped up on cushions for four days and nights. "No Robin, I am not well," she said to Sir Robert Carey, and sighed deeply many times, as she had not sighed, he said, since the death of Mary Queen of Scots. Her fingers, formerly wonderfully tapering and elegant, were grown so swollen that her coronation ring had to be cut off. Finally she was persuaded to bed, and she died at Richmond Palace on 24th March 1603.

CHAPTER EIGHT

Stuarts, Commonwealth and Restoration

*"Hampton Court is a royal pleasure house . . . built with
wonderfully great magnificence, in a plain near the Thames, of
bricks, with many towers round it."*

Ernest, Duke of Saxe-Weimer, 1613

Sir Robert Carey immediately took horse and rode north with
amazing speed to Edinburgh. King James was staying at Holyrood
Palace; Carey arrived at night and was admitted to the royal bedroom, and there he knelt and saluted him "King of England, Scotland, France and Ireland".

The King came south and was crowned at Westminster on 25th
July 1603. The usual coronation procession, however, was postponed until the following year, for there was a terrible outbreak
of plague (over a thousand people dying in London that week).
It was a pouring wet day, and the ceremony over, the Court lost
no time in moving to the comparative safety of Hampton Court.

It had to be admitted that the new king was not prepossessing
in appearance. He had weak legs, a thin beard, rolling eyes and
a tongue so big for his mouth that he was always dribbling. He
was terrified of being assassinated, and wore thickly padded
clothes that no dagger could easily penetrate. Equally he was
terrified of illness; whether it was the generally prevalent plague,
or whether it was one of his family who was laid low, James
invariably made himself scarce. He is said never to have washed,
not even his hands.

One of his first acts as king of England was to boost the royal
exchequer by the sale of knighthoods, baronetcies and other
honours. At an investiture held on 21st July 1603 in the Great
Hall at Hampton Court he created eleven peers. The fees the

recipients were required to pay were considerable – for a baron-etcy as much as £1,000.

Since the plague in London showed little sign of abating, the King decided to spend the Christmas season of 1603–4 at Hampton Court. With him came his queen, Anne of Denmark. Anne was a plump, plain, sharp-nosed woman, inclined to be lethargic, feather-brained but amiable. On the whole she was more popular than her cantankerous husband. Arabella Stuart, the King's cousin, remarked in a letter to the Earl of Shrewsbury, "If ever there were such a virtue as courtesy at the Court, I marvel what is become of it, for I protest I see little or none of it, but in the Queen."

Queen Anne was particularly fond of dancing, and it was at her suggestion that the climax of the festivities that Christmas should be a masque in which she and her ladies could take part. It was entitled "The Vision of the Twelve Goddesses". Samuel Daniel wrote the words and the scenery was by Inigo Jones. The costumes were to be provided by ransacking and adapting the dresses of Elizabeth I, which were sent for from the Tower.

As well as this masque there were plays and entertainments every night; the King's Company of Players, including Shakespeare, were among the performers, and on New Year's night there was a "play of Robin Goodfellow and a mask brought in by a magician of China".

On Twelfth Night there was a Scottish sword dance, as well as another play; then the King went into his Presence Chamber and lost the huge sum of £500 at dice – which put him off gambling for a while.

The Queen's masque was performed on the following Sunday (8th January) in the presence of the whole Court, the Spanish and Polish ambassadors and their suite, and many of the followers of the ambassadors from Florence and Savoy – not, however, the ambassadors themselves who had quarrelled so much about who should take precedence that both of them stayed away. Perhaps it was as well that not quite everybody attended, for the Great Hall, remarked Dudley Carleton in a letter to his friend John Chamberlain (15th January 1604), "was much lessened by the works that were in it . . . . At the upper end, near the dais, was constructed a temple while the other was made into a rock, and in several places, the waits placed, in attire like savages; through the midst from the top came winding stair of breadth of three to march, and so descended the maskers by three and three . . . the best presentation I have at any time seen."

The festivities ended with a banquet which, not starting until after midnight, must have gone on far into the small hours. Queen Anne had been accustomed to very lengthy meals; in the Danish court a banquet might last as long as seven hours, and by comparison the English were thought to bolt their food. A "full service", i.e. a princely feast, comprised thirty-two dishes, including salads of various kinds, fried dishes and tansies (an elaborate form of scrambled egg, with cream, spices, spinach, walnut-tree buds and sugar), hot and cold meats, different sorts of poultry, game-birds such as teal, snipe and partridge, then larger birds like peacocks, bittern and swans, followed by marrow-bone pie, quince pie and florentines. Banquets often began with a dish which was purely for show, and sweetmeats such as marzipan and preserved fruits were eaten at intervals throughout the meal. Wines were commonly from Bordeaux, or the Rhine, then there was Sack (a dry sherry), Muscadine, Malmsey and Osey. Osey was white wine diluted with water and white of egg and flavoured with bay, salt, aniseed, peppers, coriander and liquorice.

At such masques as "The Vision of the Twelve Goddesses", King James enjoyed himself well enough as a spectator, but what he really liked was hunting. "Sometimes he comes to Counsell", wrote Thomas Wilson in a letter to Sir Thomas Parry (June 1603), "but most tyme he spends in the Feildes and Parkes and Chases, chasing away idleness by violent exercise and early rysing."

However, he was a complex character, and loved debating, especially in Latin and would enter into an argument simply to show off his thought-processes.

It was perhaps for this reason that he took part himself in the Hampton Court Conference (14th–16th January 1604), a religious discussion to settle the differences between the Puritans and the

Church of England. The Puritans were petitioning that the ring should no longer be used in the marriage service, nor the sign of the cross in baptism, and that clergy should cease to wear vestments, even the surplice being made optional.

The Book of Common Prayer had been drawn up in the reign of Edward VI. The King called this conference to decide how far Puritan objections to it were justified, also to consider the matters of excommunication and the finding of clergy for Ireland, and to settle various knotty problems posed by James himself. To it came the Privy Council, the Archbishop of Canterbury, eight bishops, eight deans and two doctors of divinity, as well as four spokesmen for the Puritans, headed by a Dr Reynolds. All decisions taken at the conference depended ultimately on the side taken by the King himself; as it progressed it became clear that his sympathies lay far more with the Anglicans than with the Puritans. "My Lords," he said, turning to the bishops, "if once you were out, and they in, I know not what would become of my supremacy; for *no bishop*, no king."

Consequently the Puritans were obliged to conform to the guidelines laid down by the established Church, or else lose their livings. The Archbishop of Canterbury was overjoyed:
"Undoubtedly your Majesty speaks by the special assistance of God's Spirit," he pronounced; but afterwards John Harington [Elizabeth I's godson] criticized the unbridled language the King had used during the proceedings and commented that "the spirit was rather foule mouthed".

The most lasting result of the Hampton Court Conference, however, was the compilation of the King James or Authorized Version of the Bible. The making of a new translation was proposed, rather tentatively, by Dr Reynolds; in this he gained the full support of the King, who decreed that the work should be done by the most learned men in the universities of Oxford and Cambridge, then reviewed by the Bishops, shown to the Privy Council and lastly put before James himself for his approval. The translation thus undertaken was completed in 1611, and the King pronounced that this version, and no other, was to be used in churches throughout the land.

The conference ended, the King left Hampton Court to go hunting at Royston, thence to London for the postponed coronation procession. His elder son, Henry, then eleven years old and not yet Prince of Wales, came independently to the Palace and stayed there througout the summer. He was a popular boy, slim, auburn haired, with a healthy outdoor complexion – the result of all his sporting activities. He was an excellent tennis-player, and also enjoyed hunting, tilting, archery and swimming. Hampton Court gave him scope to practise all these, and he was still at the Palace when the King and Queen returned in the autumn. It became the custom for the Court to spend the early part of September at Windsor and then move on to Hampton Court where King and Queen were joined by lords and ladies who had spent the summer on their country estates. They would stay there until October, attended by a great crowd of servants and hangers-on – so many that often they could not all be accommodated in the Palace but camped in tents around the gates.

The brother of Queen Anne was Christian IV, King of Denmark, and in the summer of 1606 he was invited to come on a state visit to England. He arrived with a bodyguard a hundred strong, all dressed in blue velvet. King James wanted to impress his brother-in-law, who was entertained and shown the sights. Great feasts were held, and the Danes consumed enormous quantities of wine. Then James took Christian on a tour of his palaces, Richmond, Windsor and Hampton Court. At each, entertainment and feasting were provided. When they came to Hampton Court, the two kings were regaled with a performance of (apparently) *Macbeth*, given by the King's Company of Players including, almost certainly, Shakespeare. Rehearsals were held in the Great Watching Chamber, and the actors entered the Hall through the Screens Passage.

In common with her husband, Queen Anne never cared much for London; but while he would go off hunting whenever he could to Royston or Newmarket, she preferred to retreat to Oatlands or Hampton Court. From 1615 her health began to decline, and she was no longer able to dance as she loved to do, for she had dropsy and her legs were swollen. She tried taking the waters

Henry, Prince of Wales, in the Hunting Field
Painting possibly by Robert Peake and dating from 1606–7. The Prince's companion is the Earl
of Essex.

at Bath but to no effect, and she became ill again in the autumn of 1617. She said herself that it was nothing but gout; but the trouble was more serious, described by John Chamberlain as "an yll habit or disposition thorough her whole body". After Christmas she retired to Oatlands, where she was visited secretly by Roman Catholic priests. At Hampton Court in October she suffered a severe heart attack, nearly choking in her own blood. During November and December she continued ill, and was not fit enough to join the King at Whitehall for Christmas. However she attended a lengthy sermon by the Bishop of London at Hampton Court (in a room adjoining the Paradise Chamber) so her life was not despaired of yet. The King came down twice a week to see her. But by the end of February she was clearly very ill. Prince Charles* arrived to be with her, and the Archbishop of Canterbury repeatedly tried to persuade her to make her will. The Queen put off the task for she refused to believe that her end was near. She suggested to the Prince that he should go home. "No," he replied, "I will wait upon your Majesty." At about one o'clock in the morning of 2nd March, her sight failed, and three hours later she gave "five or six little groans" and died. Her body was eviscerated and on 6th March was taken by barge to Somerset House for a prolonged lying in state.

King James bore her death with equanimity and only a month after her funeral appeared arrayed in a new suit of pale blue satin. He continued to make regular visits to Hampton Court, coming there every September, as was his custom, until his death in 1625.

––––––––––––––––––––

The famous architect and designer Inigo Jones had been made surveyor of the King's Works in 1615, and shortly after James's death made the following notes in his copy of Palladio (the man whose works had influenced him most),
"The First Court [originally Cloister Green] of Hampton Court is 166 fo. square. The Seconde Fountaine Court [now Clock Court] is 92 fo. broade and 150 fo. longe. The Greene Court is 108 fo. broade, and 116 fo. longe, the walkes on cloysters at 14 fo. between the walles. September the 28th 1625."

111

* His elder brother Henry was already dead; this sporting and popular prince had suffered what appears to have been a brain tumour and had died on 12th November 1612 at the age of 18.

In the latter years of James's reign, negotiations were taking place for his heir Charles to marry the daughter of the King of Spain. Consequently preparations were made to entertain the Spanish ambassador Count Gondomar, and it was proposed that he should be lodged at Hampton Court in the Palace itself. This was an exceptional favour but the ambassador objected because the proffered rooms were not in the main building and were entirely lacking in furniture. In the end the negotiations for the Spanish marriage fell through, and it was arranged that Charles should marry Henrietta Maria, the daughter of the King of France.

The wedding took place shortly after Charles's accession, and because there was once again plague in London the young couple came to spend part of their honeymoon at Hampton Court. They arrived on 6th July 1625. The bride was very young, only fifteen years old, and she came surrounded with a group of over a hundred courtiers, including ladies-in-waiting, two ambassadors and about thirty Roman Catholic priests. This French court within the English court, arrogant as some of its members were (particularly one of the Queen's ladies, Madame de St Georges), stirred up much ill feeling. The young queen naturally liked to have her compatriots and co-religionists around her; but their presence was resented by Charles who, after delivering certain threats through his favourite, the Duke of Buckingham, ("Queens of England have been beheaded before now!") finally resolved to send them all packing back across the Channel. On 7th August he wrote to the Duke,

"I command you to send all the Frenche away by tomorrow out of Towne. If you can, by faire meanes . . . otherwise, force they away, dryving them away like so many wylde beasts, until ye have shipped them, and so the Devil goe with them. Lett me heare no answer, but of the performance of my command. So I rest

Your faithful constant loving friend
Charles R.''

Although this matter was for some time a bone of contention between the French and the English, Charles remained adamant and made very few concessions, not even when the French envoy Bassonpierre came to plead with him at Hampton Court Palace. "Imagine my grief," wrote Bassonpierre, "that the Queen of Great Britain has the pain of viewing my departure, without being of any service to her."

So Henrietta Maria was deprived of her companions, and doubtless shed very few tears when her old enemy the Duke of Buckingham was assassinated on 23rd August 1628

Charles continued to use Hampton Court Palace at different times during the following years, and particularly when plague was raging in London. For this reason he came in the summer of 1636. An attempt was made to isolate the Palace; no one from London was allowed to come within ten miles of it, and there were restrictions on river traffic. Despite these precautions, the disease broke out in Kingston and Teddington.

The Court stayed on at the Palace until Christmas, and they were entertained by performances of plays every few days from the 17th November until the 24th January, the repertoire including *"The Moore of Venice"* and *"Hamlett"*.

In 1638–9 Charles initiated certain improvements to the Palace and its grounds. Notably he had a channel cut eleven miles long and twenty-one feet wide to bring water from the Colne River at Longford across Hounslow Heath as far as Hampton Court, where it would supply the ponds and fountains. The cost of this was £4,102. At the same time he adorned the gardens with statues, and the walls of the Palace with works of art.*

The turning-point of Charles's fortunes was probably his ill-judged attempt to arrest five members of Parliament (4th February 1642), which put London in such a turmoil that the King abruptly left the city, and fled with the royal family to Hampton Court. Their coming was so totally unexpected that he, the Queen and the three eldest children had to sleep all in one room.

Five years later Charles was back, but as a prisoner. By then the Queen had returned to her native France (spending one night at the Palace on the way to embarking at Dover). After the Battle

113

* Including the Mantegna *Triumph of Caesar* and the Raphael Cartoons, but for further details see the Appendix.

Charles I and Henrietta Maria
departing for the Chase.
By Daniel Mytens, c. 1630–32.
In the bottom left-hand corner
is the royal dwarf Sir Jeffrey
Hudson, made to appear even
more diminutive so as to give
the King greater stature.

of Naseby it was clear that the Royalist cause was lost. The Palace was taken over by Parliamentarians, who destroyed both the altar-piece and the stained glass in the Chapel Royal. In 1646 Charles, who had been besieged at Oxford, fled to Newark, surrendered, fell into the hands of Cromwell's Model Army, and finally (24th August 1647) was brought as a prisoner to Hampton Court.

It was more in the nature of house-arrest than strict imprisonment. Colonel Whalley and a troop of soldiers were there to guard him, yet he had his servants to look after him, he was allowed to move about the Palace at will, and to see his children who were lodged at Syon House. He dined in the Presence Chamber, and afterwards gentlemen were allowed to kiss the royal hand. One of these was the diarist John Evelyn:

"I came to Hampton Court, where I had the honour to kisse his Majesty's hand, he being in the power of those execrable villains who not long after murdered him." (10th October 1647)

Oliver Cromwell also came, and conversed with Charles in the garden. It is possible that if the King had consented to come to terms with him, he would have been reinstated to something approaching his former power, or at least to a modified form of monarchy. But Charles, clinging to his belief in the divine right of kings, refused to compromise, and Cromwell finally abandoned the negotiations.

The King had the impression, whether true or not, that there was going to be an attempt by the Levellers to assassinate him.* He therefore decided to escape. On 11th November 1647 he spent most of the day shut up in his chamber writing letters; he had commanded that he should not be interrupted. He called for a candle when it grew dark (it was a particularly dark and stormy evening), but he did not attend prayers at five o'clock as he usually did. At seven o'clock Colonel Whalley, growing "extreme restless" in his thoughts, peered through the keyhole, but could not see any sign of the King. Then they forced open the door and found nothing but the King's cloak on the floor and three letters left on the table. The back door was open, and, accompanied by Colonel Legge, Charles had crept down the back

---

* This idea had also occurred to Cromwell, who had written to Colonel Whalley advising him to be vigilant.

stairs, passed through the gallery to the room called "Paradise", thence to the river, which he crossed and rode with his followers Berkeley and Ashburnham, first to Oatlands and then to Southampton. From there they sailed to the Isle of Wight, where they made their way to Carisbrooke Castle. It is not entirely clear why Charles chose to go to Carisbrooke, except that the governor of the island, Robert Hammond (a relation of Cromwell's) was said to be somewhat sympathetic to the Royalist cause, and the King may therefore have thought it would be a good base from which to negotiate.

Cromwell, however, had ceased to trust him, and now sided with the Levellers. Charles was kept at the castle in stricter imprisonment, and finally, after the bitter struggle of the Second Civil War, he was brought up to London for his trial and executed outside his own palace at Whitehall in January 1649.

Parliament decreed that an inventory, with valuations, should be made of all the property and collections of "the late Charles Stuart". Two trustees were appointed, John Humphreys and John Belchamp, and the intention was that everything should be sold, in the first place to defray the King's and Queen's debts. The 332 paintings then at Hampton Court Palace were assessed at a total value of £4,675. 16s. 6d. – of which the Mantegna *Triumph of Caesar* was valued at £1,000 and the Raphael Cartoons at £300. The tapestries in the Palace were put at a rather higher rate, the *Story of Abraham* series, for instance, being valued at £8,260.

A complete survey was now undertaken of the Palace buildings, with the purpose of determining their demolition value; this was set at £7,777. 13s. 15d., and the site worth a yearly rental of £36. The parks were also valued, and were rated at £1,204 a year. The whole Palace might well have been demolished, only it was decided to reward the victorious Cromwell by offering him a suite of rooms there. At first he declined this, and it was once again resolved that the Palace and parks should be put up for sale. The survey was not finished until 5th April 1653. On 6th December of that year Cromwell was created Lord Protector. As a result he no longer felt it inappropriate that he should reside

in a royal palace, and he decided to use it as a country-house.

Together with his wife Joan, Cromwell virtually held court there, and was addressed as "Highness". While most of Charles's art collection was sold, Cromwell decided that the Mantegna paintings and the Raphael Cartoons should be reserved to continue to adorn the walls. Once John Milton the poet came and played the organ to him in the Chapel. At other times he amused himself by hunting in the parks. On the whole he ate frugally, but every Monday he dined with the army officers and there was much crude and uproarious horseplay, he "shewed them a hundred Antick Tricks, as throwing of cushions, and putting live coals into their pockets and boots . . . taking drink freely, and opening himself every way to the most free familiarity . . . sometimes before he had half dined, he would give order for a

Hampton Court Palace from the river.
c. 1640. Artist unknown. The Palace has changed very little from the 16th-century view on page 94, except that the line of the Great Hall roof is now flat. There was still no bridge over the Thames; a flat-bottomed ferry may be seen on the left.

drum to beat, and call on his foot Guards, like a kennel of hounds, to snatch off meat from his table and tear it in pieces. . .'' (Heath: *Flagellum*). In short, Cromwell was hardly the old sober-sides one tends to think of him!

His daughter Mary was married in the Chapel to Viscount Falconbridge in November 1657, and the ceremony was performed by one of Cromwell's chaplains. But perhaps because he was afraid that the validity of the wedding might later be doubted, he raised no objection to their being married all over again according to the Anglican rites, by a certain Dr Hewitt.

Cromwell may have realized that the Commonwealth regime could not long survive his own death. He used Hampton Court more and more as a retreat from the worries of state affairs. Much to his distress his favourite daughter Elizabeth became seriously

119

ill. He was up in London but rushed back to Hampton Court
to be with her; it is alleged that the dying girl pleaded with him
to restore the monarchy. Then Cromwell himself fell ill; his doctors did not expect him to live. "I declare to you", he said to
them, "that I shall not die of this illness, of this I am certain
. . . God Himself has vouchsafed this answer to our prayers."
He did indeed seem to recover, but relapsed again. In the end
he was taken to Whitehall, as it was thought the air might suit
him better there, but after a few days he died; this was on the
night of 2nd September 1658.

After his death, Oliver Cromwell was succeeded briefly as Protector by his elder son Richard. It was found that the elder Cromwell
had incurred debts amounting to £29,000. To defray these it was
once more suggested that the contents of Hampton Court should
be sold. The idea was also to render the Palace more or less unin-
habitable for Richard, and to prevent this and other royal palaces
"from becoming objects of desire by ambitious men". However
the Palace contents were not sold and all was at a standstill for
about six months, when it was offered to General Monck. However, the General, who was one of those most active in bringing
about the restoration of the monarchy, regarded this as a ruse
to make him fall foul of Charles Stuart, and he therefore refused.

From late 1659 there had been a growing public demand that
there should be a king once more at the head of state affairs;
and in the eyes of Royalists, Charles II's reign had begun on the
day of his father's execution in 1649. The younger Charles spent
most of his years in exile in France. In 1650 he sailed to Scotland
to rally his supporters there and was crowned King of Scotland
at Scone. He marched south, but his army was defeated by Cromwell near Worcester; after this he became a fugitive with a price
of £1,000 on his head. Being an unusually tall man, he was difficult to disguise. But dressed in rough clothes, with his hair cut
and his face blackened with soot, he was hidden by William
Penderel in an oak-tree in the grounds of Boscobel House.

After the Restoration, he had iron firebacks made for Hampton
Court commemorating the famous Boscobel Oak.

From Boscobel, Charles moved to Bristol, thence to Brighton and sailed back to the Continent. After the death of Oliver Cromwell, General Monck (then commander of the army in Scotland) pressed for the resignation of Richard and the recalling of Charles.* Charles agreed that if he were made king there should be liberty of worship, the army were to be paid in full including all arrears, and there should be a free pardon for all those involved in the Civil War, with the exception of the regicides.

Charles was an athletic man, and very fond of tennis. Henry VIII's old court at the Palace had fallen into disrepair, and one of the first improvements Charles II made there was to have it restored and refurbished with "netts, curtains and lynes . . . covering of seats with velvet cushions and other necessaries." The lines were cut out of black marble. On 21st January 1661 a certain Stephen Charlton recorded,

"The King is in very good health and goes to Hampton Court often, and back again the same day, but very private. Most of his exercise is in the Tennis Court in the morning, when he doth not ride abroad; and when he doth ride abroad, he is on horseback by break of day, and most commonly back before noon."

At Hampton Court, Charles set in hand various improvements. The Astronomical Clock was repainted, the stables repaired, and a number of very fine yew trees were planted. He undertook the laying out of Home Park with its avenue of limes, the digging of the canal known as the Long Water, and the restocking of all the parks with game. He granted to the neighbouring town of Kingston the right to hold a weekly market and, in exchange for land given to the Crown, a fat buck every year from Hampton Court Park.

The diarist Samuel Pepys visited the Palace on 12th May 1662, when he and his party were shown over the whole building by Mr Marriot the housekeeper. He describes it as "indeed nobly furnished, particularly the Queen's bed, given her by the states of Holland; a looking-glasse sent by the Queene-mother from France, hanging in the Queen's chamber, and many brave pictures."

Hampton Court was at this time being prepared for the recep-

---

* Monck was rewarded with the stewardship of Hampton Court and Park for life, together with the sum of £20,000.

Interior of Royal Tennis Court. The court was originally made for Henry VIII in 1529–30, but extensively restored for Charles II. The game is still played there, and spectators may watch from the gallery on the right. William and Mary's monogram ornaments the wall on the left.

tion of Catherine of Braganza. She had sailed from Lisbon, and two days after Samuel Pepys's visit arrived at Portsmouth; after about a week she came ashore, met Charles and was married to him the next day. The new Queen had come escorted by a bevy of Portuguese ladies-in-waiting. Pepys found ''nothing in them that is pleasing''; they were ugly women in strange old-fashioned farthingales. John Evelyn had a poor opinion of them too; ''never,'' he wrote in his diary, ''had a pack of such hideous, odious disagreeable women been gathered together to attend a Queen.''

The honeymoon was to be spent at Hampton Court, and the royal couple arrived on 29th May. The Queen, though not handsome, turned out to be rather better-looking than many people had expected. Admittedly she had protruding teeth and was somewhat short; still, as Charles declared, there was nothing about her "that in the least degree can shock one ... I think I must be the worst person living (which I hope I am not) if I be not a good husband."

Unfortunately the King's idea of being a good husband did not entirely coincide with the Queen's. Not called the Merry Monarch for nothing, he had in his time numerous mistresses and fourteen acknowledged bastards (who were incidentally a considerable drain on his finances). His principal mistress for many years was Barbara Villiers, Lady Castlemaine. The evening that Catherine of Braganza arrived at Portsmouth Charles spent at her house, and there (Pepys was told by his wife), "the King and she did send for a pair of scales and weighed one another; and she, being with child, was said to be the heaviest." The child was, of course, the King's. Lady Castlemaine threatened that she would give birth to the baby at Hampton Court, just at the time of the royal honeymoon. Charles, however, wanted to have his mistress appointed to the royal household, so she did nothing so embarrassing, and the child was born in London. She then moved to her uncle's house at Richmond.

The Queen fell ill (her constitution was never strong) and it was thought she might be sickening for smallpox. She complained bitterly about the English food, and even more about the English drinking water.

When she was somewhat recovered, the King decided to introduce Lady Castlemaine to her. Catherine was seated in the Presence Chamber at Hampton Court, when in she came, led by Charles, and kissed the Queen's hand. At first the Queen stood up and received her graciously, but then she realized who she was – she had already been warned of Charles's predeliction in that direction. Abruptly Catherine sat down, turned pale, burst into tears, bled from the nose and fainted.

Her husband took this as a display of bad temper, and complained to the Earl of Clarendon of her lack of affability. He also criticized her Portuguese attendants, who clearly would never be integrated with the English Court. Clarendon did what he could to make peace; he suggested to the Queen that infidelity was at least as common in Portugal as in this country. But the Queen protested tearfully "that she had not expected her husband to be already engaged in his affection to another lady", and she would not hear of Barbara Villiers being admitted to her household. Clarendon put it to Charles that although it might be acceptable on the Continent for kings to keep mistresses at court, it would never be tolerated in this country. Charles, however, had entertained "the lady" at Hampton Court only the previous evening and he never wanted people to say of him that he was a man ruled by his wife. He decided to send Catherine's attendants back to Portugal, and when she threatened that if he did she would go too, he said that he doubted if her mother would have her. Charles had his way, and all but the elderly Countess of Penalva, some priests, musicians and kitchen-maids, were promptly returned to Lisbon. (One of the ladies, Pepys was told, had "dropped a child" since the Queen's coming to Hampton Court, "and the King would not have them searched, whose it is.") He would have liked to have sent the musicians too, for the sounds they produced were cacophonous.

Charles was still determined that Barbara Castlemaine should become a lady of the Queen's bedchamber. He persuaded the Earl of Clarendon to act for him, writing that anyone who tried to thwart his wishes in this respect would find the King had become his life-long enemy. The Queen protested, but was forced in the end to agree. Lady Castlemaine was given rooms at Hampton Court, and Catherine had no option but to receive her with as good grace as she could muster.

Before the King and Queen left Hampton Court on 23rd August, they were visited by Henrietta Maria, now Queen-mother. King Charles and his brother James had to act as interpreters, for Henrietta could speak no Portuguese or Spanish, and Catherine not a word of French. The royal party left in a ceremonial river procession down the Thames to London. John Evelyn described the scene in his diary; "innumerable boats and vessels, dressed and adorned with all imaginable pomp, but above all the thrones, arches, pageants, and other representations, stately barges of the Lord Mayor and companies . . . in my opinion it far exceeded

Barbara Villiers, Duchess of Cleveland
Costumed as Minerva, one of the 'Windsor Beauties' series painted by Sir Peter Lely *c.* 1665.
The lady was the principal mistress of Charles II and bore him at least six children. She was
given lodgings at the Palace.

125

The Miraculous Draught of Fishes
One of the Raphael Cartoons, bought by Charles I and now at the Victoria and Albert Museum.
Intended for tapestry, the design is reversed, so that Christ is shown blessing with his left hand.

all Venetian Bucentoras etc. on the Ascension, whom they go to espouse the Adriatic."

In describing the Palace, Evelyn took particular note of the fountain adorned with statues which he says were by Fanelli. The fountain also caught the eye of aristocratic visitors such as the Duc de Monconys; he wrote that over the marble basin and fountain were "four syrens in bronze, seated astride on dolphins, between which was a shell, supported on the foot of a goat". Above them were four little children, seated and each holding a fish, and above all a large statue of a woman. This is the so-called Diana Fountain, now in Bushey Park.

The Palace was also visited (1669) by Cosimo, Duke of Tuscany. He had to admit it was picturesque: "although the more elegant orders of architecture are not to be found in it . . . yet it is, on the whole, a beautiful object to the eye. The numerous towers or cupolas, judiciously disposed at irregular distances all over the vast pile of building, form a most striking ornament to it, whether viewed near or at a distance."

The King came seldom however, in the latter part of his reign. He was there in the summer of 1665 because of the plague which was very prevalent in London. Work was done at this time on Lady Castlemaine's rooms, to embellish them further. Samuel Pepys came there on 23rd July and attended service in the Chapel. He was a little dismayed that he did not seem expected to dinner anywhere, but ended up dining, congenially after all, with Lely the painter. Lely had been commissioned by the Duchess of York to portray the young ladies of the Court, three-quarter length – the series of langorous and voluptuous ladies now known as the *Windsor Beauties* – and this doubtless accounted for his presence in the Palace.

The King and Queen, retreating further from the plague, left Hampton Court for Salisbury and then Oxford. By the end of January 1666 they were back, and were again visited by Samuel Pepys and John Evelyn – the King thanking them for their good service, for they had remained at their duties in London throughout the months when the plague was at its height.

Charles and the Court remained for a week and then returned

127

to Whitehall. He would occasionally visit the Palace, as at the
time of his mother's death in 1669, but never stayed long. When
his brother James succeeded him as king, Hampton Court was
used even less. There is a solitary instance of a Council being
held on 29th May 1687, when "the militia was put down and
the licensing of ale-houses was put in other hands than the justi-
ces of the peace".

CHAPTER NINE

William and Mary

"Whoever knew Hampton Court before it was begun to be rebuilt, or altered, by the late King William, must acknowledge it was a very complete palace before, and fit for a king; and though it might not, according to the modern method of building or of gardening, pass for a thing exquisitely fine, yet it . . . showed a situation exceedingly capable of improvement, and of being made one of the most delightful palaces in Europe."

Daniel Defoe (1660?–1731)
A Tour through the Whole Island of Great Britain
Letter 3, London to Land's End.

By his first wife, Anne Hyde, James II had two surviving daughters, Mary and Anne. At the age of fifteen Mary, despite her protests and her father's disapproval, was married to William Prince of Orange. William himself was the son of another Stuart Mary, the sister of Charles II and James II; the couple were thus first cousins.

After the death of Anne Hyde, James took a second wife, Mary Beatrice of Modena, thereby committing himself even more irrevocably to Roman Catholicism and gaining the approval of the King of France as well as the Pope. Both James's wives were troubled with repeated miscarriages*, but at last in the autumn of 1688 it was announced that Mary had given birth to a healthy son, and the boy was christened James Francis Edward. Extreme Anglican opinion was shocked at the thought that the baby would take precedence over his half-sisters and that the reign of James would be followed by that of another Catholic monarch. It was rumoured that the child was not James's at all, but had been smuggled into Mary's bed in a warming-pan.

A secret message was sent to William of Orange from seven dignitaries including the Bishop of London, inviting him to invade England. William set about making preparations but delayed sailing until he was reasonably certain that there was

129

---

* It is possible that James may have had syphilis. He was certainly a dissolute man, and the unhappy pattern of repeated stillbirths and miscarriages was carried on into the next generation, Mary in the end childless, and all but one of Anne's seventeen or eighteen children dying in infancy.

William III
After Sir Peter Lely

Mary II
After W. Wissing

no immediate danger of Holland being invaded by France. He finally set sail on 1st November 1688 and landed at Torbay on the 5th. He advanced steadily towards London and, as he did so, many of James's principal officers went over to his side. James himself, fearing that he might meet the same fate as his father had – for feeling was running very strongly against him – took ship and fled to France. His daughter Anne had already left the Palace (Mary of course was in Holland), followed on 10th December by Mary Beatrice who with her baby son escaped by boat travelling from Gravesend to Calais. William was at Abingdon when he heard of the King's flight; he then rode via Windsor to London and held court at St James's Palace. King James's action was taken to mean that he had abdicated and the country had no sovereign. Mary was then invited to become queen with her husband as prince-consort; but she refused, saying it would ''set up a divided interest'' between them. As for William, he declared that if he were not made king he would leave the country for ever. So a compromise was arranged, and at the Banqueting House at Whitehall (where forty years earlier their grandfather had been executed) the two were proclaimed jointly king and queen.

Queen Mary was much loved and admired. She was slender and exceptionally tall, her dark hair contrasting with her pale, transparent complexion. Admittedly her eyes protruded slightly and her cheeks were rather full, but her mouth and throat were beautiful and her manners "full of sweetness and majesty".*

William, on the other hand, was unprepossessing. About five inches shorter than his wife, he was thin and weakly with great dark eyes. Most people found him dry, brusque and totally lacking in charm – though his wife was unswervingly loyal, even when he neglected her, and ultimately learned to love him. He spoke shortly and was often bad-tempered and irritable, especially when, forced to stay in town, he could not pursue his favourite sport of hunting. He excelled at this, and at soldiery – he was very much a "man's man" – and his powers of endurance were considerable, despite his poor health and stooping physique. He suffered from asthma all his life. When Mary arrived from Holland to join him as queen (12th February 1689), she found him "in a very ill condition . . . a violent cough upon him and . . . extremely lean".

Because of the King's poor health, the couple almost immediately left London and came down to Hampton Court – first for a few days, then for a longer stay the following month. They found the place delightful. It must have reminded William of Holland, the flat terrain, the avenues of limes and the canal nearby; moreover there were spacious parks where he could go hunting. Mary too was charmed with it. She ferreted around, turning up the quilts and looking into cupboards, "as people do when they come to an inn," remarked her companion the Duchess of Marlborough. She loved the gardens as well, and used to walk five or six miles a day on her tours of inspection in the Palace grounds. She seems to have had some misgivings about being made queen, for she wrote "My heart is not made for a

* Daniel Bourdon: *Mémoires de Monsieur de Bourdon*

kingdom and my inclination leads me to a quiet life"; but she was very happy to be reunited with William, and relieved to find he was determined to shoulder all burdens of government. So she chatted to everybody, and smiled her welcome to the throngs of people who came to see her at Hampton Court.

Among those who flocked to the Palace were sick people suffering from scrofula or the "King's Evil". It was thought that the King, just because he *was* King, could cure the disease by simply touching them. William was scornful, "it is a silly superstition," he said in his heavy Dutch accent, "give the poor creatures some money and let them go." This break with tradition did nothing to increase his popularity, nor did his dismissal of the musicians from the Chapel Royal, nor the way he insisted on wearing his hat during church services.

London may have been a small city by modern standards, but the atmosphere was extremely polluted, chiefly from the burning of coal fires. A Frenchman visiting in 1690 described it as full of "vapours, fogs and rains" which "drag with them in their fall the heaviest particles of the smoke; this forms black rain and produces the ill effects that may justly be expected of it." Clearly this was no place for an asthmatic like William, and he felt it essential that the main royal residence should be somewhere healthier than the crowded, blackened, noisome Palace of Whitehall.

Although William and Mary considered the location of Hampton Court pleasing, and the air so good that they decided to spend some months in every year there, they found fault with the building. The old Tudor structure was not to their taste. They wanted something much more impressive, on the lines of the French King's Palace of Versailles, and at the same time more comfortable, like the Dutch palaces of Het Loo and Huis ten Bosch. Also their joint sovereignty meant they needed a palace with *two* series of state rooms, each equally splendid. Hampton Court would not suit their purpose as it was; they decided to have it converted or rebuilt. The architect they chose was Sir Christopher Wren.

Wren at this time was fifty-seven years old, a mature and established architect. Up to the age of thirty he had worked as a scientist, and was a founder-member of the Royal Society. Early works in architecture included the Sheldonian Theatre Oxford and the chapel of Pembroke College Cambridge; he visited Paris in 1668 and his later buildings were much influenced by French styles. The widespread destruction caused by the Great Fire of London afforded him considerable scope; he was commissioned to rebuild fifty-one city churches (1670–86), as well as St Paul's Cathedral (1675–1710). All this, as well as secular work, such as Chelsea Hospital (1682–92), was also preoccupying him at the same time as designing for the Palace.

Wren's original plans for Hampton Court are indicated by a series of pencil drawings. He intended to demolish the old Cloister Green on the east side of the Palace, together with the Queen's Gallery designed for Anne Boleyn, and replace them with a large new courtyard. Around this were to be grouped two series of state-rooms, the King's Side and the Queen's Side, each approached by a ceremonial staircase. Then Wren planned to erect an impressive Grand Front, culminating in a dome mounted on a convex drum (this would have replaced the old Tudor rooms overlooking the east side of the Clock Court). This front was to be ornamented with giant columns two storeys in height, between the central pair an equestrian statue (possibly of William), and above that a coat-of-arms with male and female supporters, surmounted by a crown.

Another sketch dating from about 1689 shows a proposed rebuilding of almost the entire palace. The main approach was to be a northern one from Bushey Park, and there was to be a wide entrance courtyard on this side of the Palace. Clock Court and the Tudor buildings to the west would also have been demolished to make another main axis running right through from west to east, in line with the Long Water (the canal constructed in Charles II's reign). In short, the only part of the old palace that would have been allowed to survive was Henry VIII's Great Hall. But this would have lain right across the main approach, and Wren may have intended to reface it. Judging by the plan that survives in the Sir John Soane's Museum, he seems to have proposed a new entrance in the centre of the north wall, which would have been approached by a flight of steps.

133

Fortunately, because it makes the existing Palace much more interesting – or unfortunately, because it makes it less of an architectural unity – Wren's original plans did not come to fruition. They must have proved too ambitious and had to be abandoned. In the compromise scheme that survives today much of the Tudor Palace was allowed to remain, although this meant that there was no alignment between the Gatehouse and the Long Water. The courtyard actually built (Fountain Court) is considerably smaller than the one proposed on Wren's plan, and the King's and Queen's staircases had to be fitted in asymmetrically, the King's being approached by an Ionic colonnade. On the East Front, instead of giant columns supporting a projecting triangular pediment, a much more modest scheme of eight single-storey pilasters and a much lower pediment was devised. The reason for this may well have been the shortage of stone from Portland – for the quarries there were being kept more than busy supplying what was needed for St Paul's.

When Mary first arrived from Holland in February 1689 she lived in Mary of Modena's apartments at Whitehall (also designed by Wren), but Wren was pressed to proceed quickly with the work at Hampton Court. Even before they were crowned (April) the King and Queen had installed themselves there. Building materials were ordered in June, and the foundations were laid the following month.

A few days after the coronation, William and Mary returned to Hampton Court. Mary's sister Anne was given a suite of rooms there too. She had married George of Denmark, and at this time was expecting one of her many confinements.* Between her and Mary there was never much love lost and, according to her favourite, Sarah Duchess of Marlborough, Anne was treated very uncivilly by her brother-in-law. "I could fill many sheets" wrote the formidable Sarah, "with the brutalities that were done to the Princess in this reign." She relates how the King devoured a whole dish of fresh green peas before Anne's eyes without offering her any.

William's habit of spending so much time at Hampton Court was not popular with his courtiers, who were forced to commute

* See Chapter Ten, page 147

from London for any affairs they wished to transact. The Marquis of Halifax complained of the King's "inaccessibleness and liveing so at Hampton Court altogether" which he said "at soe active a time ruined all business". Also William's standing with the general public was deteriorating fast, partly because of his standoffishness and partly because when he did make himself accessible, he was almost always bad-tempered and taciturn. Indeed, remarked Halifax, if James had been prepared to turn Protestant, the country would have had him back as king within four months.

It was his poor health that made the King so irascible and difficult. When Halifax entreated him to spend at least an occasional night at Whitehall so that business could be dealt with there, he replied flatly, "it was not to be done except he desired to see him dead." The only concession that he and Mary were prepared to make was to acquire Kensington House, which cost them 18,000 guineas. Kensington was then a country village, but being much closer to London, it was more accessible. It was at Kensington that William installed his mistress Elizabeth Villiers.

Meanwhile he and Mary pressed on with their plans for Hampton Court, and it was in this palace that they spent the whole of August and September, giving audiences there. Then the King, making some effort to appear more convivial, went off to the races at Newmarket. Betting and gambling, he lost a good deal of money and returned in no better temper to complaints that he was spending too much time away from the capital.

The King thought that the cloister around Fountain Court was too low and dark. In an attempt to lighten it, Wren made elliptical arches under the semi-circular ones. This may have weakened the structure, and was possibly the reason why a wall collapsed, killing three or four men and injuring several others. It was said that the wall had been too flimsily built. Wren was accused of being responsible for the deaths of the men, and at the enquiry which was held before the Lords of the Treasury on 19th December it was suggested that the piers of the wall were cracked and hollow. When he denied this, William Talman the Comptroller of Works said that Wren had gone round filling in the cracks

Flora
The statue, probably by Gaius Gabriel Cibber, may be found on the south side of the Palace.

135

afterwards. There was clearly something wrong with the structure, and the only further defence Wren could think of was that only three men were killed and not four. The works were then inspected; apparently no great fault was found, and Wren was allowed to continue as architect at a wage of 4s. 10d. a day. Meanwhile William Talman, who had been one of Wren's chief accusers, continued to be employed as Comptroller at 6s. 10d. a day. Then the work progressed hampered only, as the Queen remarked, by "want of money and Portland stone".

Some of the furniture William and Mary found in the old Palace they considered out of date and decided to remove it in case it "should infect ye other Goods with moths and rottenness".* The items were given to Charles Sackville Earl of Dorset, who had been Lord Chamberlain since the time of Charles II, and they were taken back to his home at Knole in Sevenoaks. At least two arm-chairs from the Palace, together with their footstools, still survive at Knole, and they are both stamped with the date 1661, the royal crown and "H.C." for Hampton Court.

While the new Palace was being constructed, the Water Gallery by the riverside was refurbished to provide a temporary home for the royal couple, in particular Queen Mary who had more time to amuse herself there while her husband was engaged in matters of state. Daniel Defoe was much taken by it and he called it "the pleasantest little thing within doors that could possibly be made, with all the little neat curious things that suited her convenience." Among the "curious things" the Queen introduced to this country were goldfish and a small breed of mastiff known as the Dutch pug. She and William also introduced

---

* The following furnishings are listed in the Lord Chamberlain's Books (22nd June 1693):

"Three paires of purple Morella hangings
Seaven peices of Crimson Damaske hangings being ye furniture of ye Q Clossett
Two Arming Chaires & two Stooles & a Carpett all suitable to ye Clossett hanging
Two Chairs of Estate one Velvet ye other Crimson Cloath of Tissue with high stooles & Foote stooles with four Cushions to them
One purple velvet Chaire Two stooles & a foot stoole 2 Cushions & one vestment of Velvett & a Carpett of the same.
Two Vestments of Crimson Velvett One Window Curtaine of Crimson Damaske Lyned with Fustian
Six Crimson Velvett Chaires

Two large Looking Glasses
Two small Persian Carpetts two large foote Carpetts of Turkey work, Six Carpetts of Turky work about four yard long
Six Maskette Carpetts
Six Turky Carpetts being old ones
Tenn Damaske Window Curtains
One Velvet Stoole
Eight Feather Bedds & Bolstere
Six downe pillows
Six Tapestry counter points
Foure paires of Tapestry hangings of ye pleasures of Cupid
Six odd peices of Tapestry hangings
Two large fine persian Carpetts

A further list in October 1693 included a billiard table, which may by the one at Knole.

the habit of drinking chocolate, which they consumed in large quantities for breakfast.

In the Water Gallery she kept her fine collection of Chinese porcelain; the technique of making true hard-paste porcelain was still unknown in Europe and consequently these pieces were extremely rare and expensive. She had cabinets made by a craftsman called Gerard Johnson in which to house them. The walls of the Water Gallery were decorated with carvings by Grinling Gibbons and hung with paintings including the famous series of Hampton Court Beauties by Kneller.* As Marie Antoinette had later at the Petit Trianon, the Queen had a dairy installed for her amusement, and there was a bathroom with a bath of white marble "made very fine, suited either to hot or cold bathing, as the season should invite." (Defoe *Tour through the Whole Island of Great Britain.*)

Mary was very fond of needlework and while her rather weak eyes permitted her would spend hours embroidering chair-covers and hangings. Alternatively she would make knotted fringe (apparently a sort of macramé) which was not such close work. She took a great interest in the gardens, in the propagation of tropical plants (under the supervision of her head-gardener Dr Plunkenet) and in the growing of orange trees. The flowerbeds were edged with box, a fashion derived from Holland. One of the Queen's favourite retreats was the pleached avenue of wych-elms still known as Queen Mary's Bower, and here she would sit doing her knotting, playing basset, or reading. She felt that her education had been neglected, except in the matter of languages – she was fluent in French and Dutch as well as English – and she set about remedying this by reading widely in all three languages, especially poetry, geography and natural history.

The main material used for the new building was again red brick, but a paler, more orange-coloured brick than the old Tudor palace; and all the details and enrichments were executed in Portland stone. As the structure rose, various artists were commissioned to ornament it. Gaius Gabriel Cibber carved low-relief figures in stone to decorate the East Front, also free-standing figures, vases and coats-of-arms. Grinling Gibbons, who in his

---

* See Appendix page 210

East Front of the Palace. From the Fountain Garden. Wren's architecture seen between the central avenue of yew trees and across the playing fountain.

early career undertook carving in stone as well as wood, also did work for the East Front. There was another stone-carver, William Emmett, who did extensive ornamentation on the Palace, and received £918. 13s. 6d. for it. Louis Laguerre was paid £86 for ornamenting the roundels on the south side of Fountain Court with paintings of the Twelve Labours of Hercules. Fresco seldom survives long in the open air, and these have darkened beyond recognition.

Laguerre's son-in-law was the French smith Jean Tijou. Tijou was a Huguenot, which may have endeared him to Protestant William. But it was perhaps through family influence that he received the commission to design the wonderfully intricate screens that border the parterre of the Fountain Garden (the actual execution of the work seems to have been done by Huntingdon Shaw), the balustrade of the King's Staircase, and also probably the pair of gates at the Lion Gate. Tijou was not paid promptly, and in 1700 the sum of £1,315 was still owing to him.

Whenever his health permitted him, William spent every summer in his native Holland, leaving his wife to manage both state and domestic affairs until his return. Then in 1690 he was away in Ireland on the campaign which culminated in the defeat of James II at the Battle of the Boyne. Although she tried to appear

happy and competent, Mary found his absences periods of great strain; "the only thing in the world one never gets used to", she said, writing to a friend in Holland in 1694. The worry and the solitude tended to affect her health; her face swelled up and her eyes troubled her. Although only thirty-two, she complained of feeling old; she was beginning to put on weight and was generally out of sorts. She went on a diet of asses' milk. When William returned that autumn his health was not good either, and his wife was even more dismayed to learn that he intended to be off to Flanders as early as possible in the new year. Then Mary, who was in a particularly run-down and depressed state, caught smallpox. She seemed to have lost all will to live; methodi-

Tijou Screen
Detail of the exquisite wrought-ironwork that borders the Fountain Garden.

139

cally she set her affairs in order and, despite – or because of – all the desperate remedies used to try and cure her (such as bleeding, and placing red-hot irons on her forehead), she died at Kensington on 28th December 1694.

William was grief-stricken. He may not have been the most attentive of husbands, and perhaps during her lifetime had never fully appreciated Mary's human qualities. But now he mourned her sincerely and repented of his misdemeanours to the extent of turning away his mistress Elizabeth Villiers. He lived a solitary existence, consoling himself only with the company of men-friends. The rebuilding of Hampton Court came virtually to a standstill, for the King had no heart for it. The Queen had not lived to see her state-rooms completed, and very little work had been done on the interior as a whole.

The Palace might have been left in this incomplete state had it not been that three years later (4th January 1698) there was a disastrous fire in the Palace of Whitehall. It is said to have been started by a Dutch servant attempting to dry some linen. The flames spread quickly, and they could not get sufficient water to put them out because the Thames was frozen. Of the whole palace nothing remained but Inigo Jones's Banqueting House.

William was not much upset, despite the destruction of such irreplaceable works of art as the Holbein wall-paintings, for he had never liked Whitehall, and it had never suited him to live there. He realized, however, that a considerable administrative centre had been lost, and commissioned Wren to design a new palace to replace it (a project which never got beyond the planning stage). Meanwhile the King resolved to make Windsor his chief centre, use Kensington Palace for relaxation, and continue after all with the rebuilding and decorating at Hampton Court.

An estimate was prepared by Wren for the fitting up of the interior, and was presented to the King on 28th April 1699; this included the completion of a gallery 117 feet long to house the Raphael Cartoons bought by Charles I,* as well as the King's Staircase, Guard Chamber and five state apartments. All the floorboards, Wren specified, were to be fixed without the use of nails.

* See Appendix page 203

The total cost of the work was estimated at £6,800. No mention was made of the Queen's rooms.

By the summer of that year Grinling Gibbons (1648–1721) was at work on the exquisitely detailed carvings in lime-wood of fruit, flowers, plants and birds which enhance the walls. Gibbons had been born in Rotterdam, but was in London by 1671 when he was discovered by the diarist John Evelyn and introduced to Charles II. He worked at Windsor as well as Hampton Court, but his greatest masterpiece is probably the decoration of the Music Room at Petworth House.

At the same time the Neapolitan artist Antonio Verrio was commissioned to design ceiling paintings and murals. Verrio (c.1640–1707) was established in Paris when he was persuaded by Charles II to come over to this country. He worked at Windsor from 1678 to 1688, and succeeded Lely as court painter in 1684. Then he decorated the walls of Chatsworth and Burghley, and started work at Hampton Court in 1699.

Carving by Grinling Gibbons. Part of the carved frieze in King William III's State Bedroom.

141

The 'Diana' Fountain. So called, now stands in Bushey Park.

He began with the ceiling of the King's State Bedroom, for which was chosen the theme of Endymion; he received £400 for it. Then he went on to paint the King's Staircase with a complex allegorical theme expressing the prosperity and plenty hoped for during this reign. The subject relates to Julian the Apostate's work *Satires on the Caesars*; Alexander the Great, representing William, is preferred by the gods to the Roman emperors, representing the Stuart claimants, and he is invited by Hercules to join with them in a celestial banquet. Verrio also painted the King's Dressing-Room with the subject of Mars and Venus; for these two works, his bill totalled £1,800.

The embellishment of the Guard Room was undertaken by the King's gunsmith Harris. He set 3,141 arms out in the same decorative patterns that may still be seen to this day, and was rewarded with a pension for his ingenuity.

The furnishings of the state-rooms included a tall bed hung with red velvet, its finials surmounted with ostrich and heron feathers, a long-case clock by Daniel Quare, barometers by Thomas Tompion, a number of fine chandeliers, and magnificent mirrors, some of them edged with blue glass (all of these may still be seen).

Repairs and alterations were also set in hand in the Great Hall, with the intention of turning it into a theatre, but this was not completed during the King's lifetime.

More work was undertaken in the gardens and parks, under the direction of the King's gardeners, George London and Henry Wise. The Broad Walk was laid out along the line of the East Front at a cost of £600. At the end of it the gate-posts were crowned with figures of cherubs by John Nost, and the so-called Diana figure was moved to provide a centre-piece for a fountain in Bushey Park. The most spectacular change was the planting out of the rectangular plot known as the Wilderness with geometric patterns of tall clipped hedges. This included "Troy Town" (an apple-shaped section with concentric hedges), and the famous Maze, roughly triangular in shape, the only part of the Wilderness which survives today in its original form.

On the opposite side of the garden the Mount, which had been

142

such a feature in Henry VIII's day, was levelled, and the old Water Gallery, which had been refurbished for Queen Mary, was stripped and pulled down. The bricks were kept for re-use, and further to the west a new Banqueting House, designed by Wren, was set up in 1700 on the foundations of an old tower. This provided the King with a pleasant riverside dining-room; the walls were decorated with paintings by Verrio and panelling of Norwegian oak.

Before the Banqueting House was put up, and possibly as an alternative to it, there was a project to build a "Trianon" (palatial villa) on the other side of the river at Thames Ditton. Drawings

The Maze
Roughly triangular in shape, it survives from the old 'Wilderness' which was entirely divided up with hedges in geometric patterns.

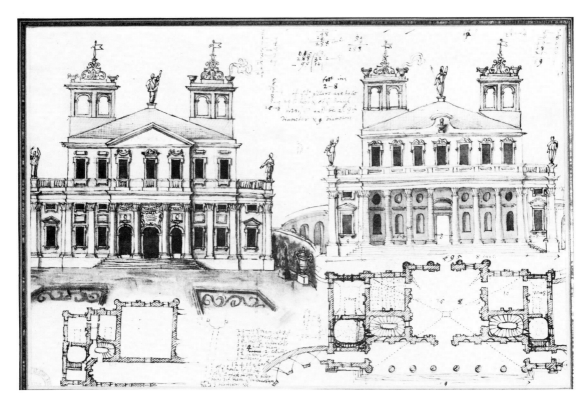

Drawings for a projected Trianon, or palatial villa, by John Talman. This is the most flamboyant of the designs executed by John and his father William with the idea of providing William III with a semi-informal retreat the other side of the river.

were made, and the site was to be in line with the most southerly of the avenues of trees which fan out from the Great Fountain Garden by the East Front. The avenue would have been continued the other side of the river, the "Trianon" completing the vista at the end of it. The intention was to provide a more or less informal retreat from the ceremonies of court life in the Palace.

The designs* were done by both William Talman (1650–1719) and his son John (1677–1726), and they date from about 1699. William Talman envisaged a rather austere building, relieved only by a central portico with a Latin inscription under the pediment (*"Vito Superba Civium Limina"*, I avoid the proud thresholds of the state). His son's designs, on the other hand, include one in a fanciful baroque style with twin turrets crowned

144

* These drawings are in the Library of the Royal Institute of British Architects; there are thirty in all.

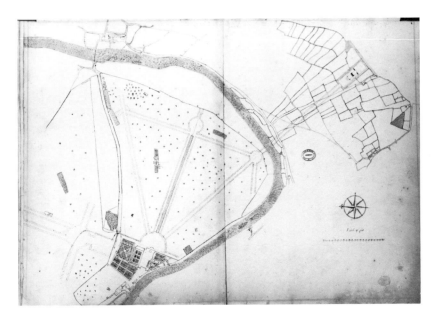

Site Plan by William Talman, showing the lay-out of the Palace and grounds in *c.* 1699, and the location of the proposed Trianon. The avenue of trees radiating from the Fountain Garden would have been continued across the river to Thames Ditton where the building was to be sited, but there was no bridge except at Kingston. The immediate surroundings of the Palace show the old Melon Ground (now glasshouses and works yard), to the side of this the Wilderness and the Tiltyards (then kitchen gardens); on the other side, by the river, the square block of the Water Gallery, which was shortly to be demolished to provide building materials for Wren's Banqueting House. To the left of the Long Water there seems to have been some sort of hunting lodge.

with gilded weather-vanes, pink marble pillars, a pitched roof, and large rhetorical statuary at the salient points. This was probably not to the King's taste; John Talman also produced a restrained classical alternative with a portico of coupled pillars and the inscription "*Parvum Parva Decent Non Regia*" (a little building is not meant for state occasions). However it was William Talman's design which seems to have been approved, at least to the extent that site plans and further drawings were done based on it. In the end, though, none of these delightful projects was actually built. The reason may have been lack of funds (the Banqueting House was obviously cheaper to build), or the problem of access (there being no bridge nearer than Kingston), or perhaps the King realized that his days were numbered.

William's health had never been particularly good, and he began to have trouble with his legs, which tended to swell up in different places. He himself thought he had dropsy. He had been a great eater, and an even greater drinker, but in the summer of 1700 he began to moderate his diet. His usual yearly visit to Holland he unwillingly postponed, and spent the month of June quietly at Hampton Court, dining privately in the Oak Room, and succumbing with some impatience to the ministrations of his doctors. He would be very well, he protested, if only they would stop prescribing for him.

The King's last visit to Holland was in summer/autumn 1701, and on his return he went straight to Hampton Court, arriving there on 5th November. The trip had been undertaken despite medical advice, and now he was in very poor state and had to be carried into the Palace. Although he recovered his health somewhat, and his temper even more (realizing that she must inevitably succeed him, he now treated Princess Anne and her husband quite civilly), he confided to a friend that he "found himself so weak he did not expect to live another summer". The main trouble was still his swollen legs. One of his more ingenious physicians invented a sort of heated box for him to sit in – this gave him some relief, but the King was too impatient to stay in it long. "I'll do what I've a mind to," he declared.

In December he moved to Kensington, in order to be nearer London for the opening of Parliament. Every Saturday, however, it was his practice to come to Hampton Court to hunt. It was on one of these Saturdays, on 21st February 1702, that his horse Sorrel tripped. A mole had raised a hillock in the otherwise flat ground of the park. The King fell off and broke his collar-bone. Not thinking that he had damaged himself seriously, he insisted on returning by coach to Kensington. With the shaking of the ride, the bone became dislodged and had to be re-set. Further swelling of the limbs followed, along with fever, coughing and nausea. The King's indifferent health had rendered the fall fatal, and he died on 8th March – leaving those loyal to the Jacobite cause* to drink the toast of the "little gentleman in black velvet", the mole who had raised the molehill in the first place.

---

* The Jacobite cause: James II had died the previous November, and the Jacobites now supported the claims of his son, James Francis Edward ('The Old Pretender').

CHAPTER TEN

Early Eighteenth Century

"Close by those meads, for ever crowned with flowers,
Where Thames with pride surveys his rising towers,
There stands a structure of majestic frame
Which from the neighbouring Hampton takes its name.
Here Britain's statesmen oft the fall foredoom
Of foreign tyrants, and of nymphs at home;
Here thou, great Anna! whom three realms obey
Dost sometimes counsel take – and sometimes tea."

Alexander Pope (1688–1744)

The Rape of the Lock, Canto I.

The great tragedy of Queen Anne's life was her failure to produce an heir to succeed her. Married to Prince George of Denmark, a man for whom, however much others may have mocked him, she had an enduring affection, she had a most unhappy history of about eighteen pregnancies. All but one of these ended in a child being born dead or surviving only briefly.

There was great celebration therefore when at Hampton Court on 24th July 1688 (the first summer of the reign of William and Mary) she was delivered of a son. Her sister was with her throughout her labour, and her brother-in-law and various courtiers actually witnessed the birth. The baby appeared healthy, and was christened four days later in the Chapel. He was named William after his uncle, who stood as godfather and declared that the boy should be known as the Duke of Gloucester. William may never have cared for Anne, but he was quick to realize that her child embodied the only hope of an English Protestant succession.

Wet-nurses were appointed, one after the other, for the baby generally refused to suck and was losing weight rapidly. Then

Mrs Wanley took over for about six weeks, but the child had terrible convulsions and a change of milk was thought desirable. The desperate search began again, many women came flocking to the Palace, since a fee of five guineas was given to every applicant. Finally Prince George discovered a Kingston woman called Mrs Pack who, though dirty and unkempt, certainly was strong and healthy. The little prince's fits ceased and he began to thrive.

Unfortunately, however, the boy developed a swelling on the head (probably hydrocephalus) and was often ill. He was lively by temperament, and enjoyed playing at soldiers with his own little army of twenty boys from Kensington, but he was subject to attacks of giddiness which no one could cure. In 1700, just after his eleventh birthday celebrations at Windsor, young William fell sick with a high fever, sore throat and vomiting. Attempts to lower the temperature by bleeding him were of no avail (and may well have been fatal) and within days the boy was dead.

Anne's grief can well be imagined. She was a reticent woman who did not often betray her feelings, but she never got over young William's death. She had no more pregnancies after this.

By the time that Anne ascended the throne, then, she had understandably lost all youthful vigour and optimism she ever had, and was a corpulent middle-aged lady much plagued with gout, who sought relief by dosing herself with laudanum. Nevertheless she was not unpopular, for she carried herself in a stately manner, spoke well and gravely, and proclaimed herself to be entirely devoted to the happiness and prosperity of her country.

At Hampton Court Palace she had the rooms of the "Queen's Side" completed for her use, including commissioning the aged Neapolitan artist Verrio to paint the walls and ceiling of the Queen's Drawing Room.* He included two (idealized) portraits of Anne, one as a figure of justice, and the other as a potentate to whom tribute was brought from all the corners of the earth. Meanwhile her husband George is there on every wall, whether as Admiral of the Fleet (inappropriately in full armour and an ermine-lined cloak) or gazing adoringly at his wife or, most ridiculously, riding a dolphin, playing an improbable harp made of shells, and, apart from a little pink drapery, entirely nude.

* By 1741 all the walls of this room were concealed with draperies of green damask, and in Queen Victoria's reign with canvas covered in flock wallpaper, neither Verrio nor the subject-matter being any longer in vogue.

Queen Anne and Prince William of Gloucester. By Sir Godfrey Kneller. The clearly ailing prince was the only one of Anne's many children to survive for any length of time. He was born at Hampton Court.

Verrio had been given rooms in the Palace – as a Roman Catholic he needed some inducement to work for these Protestant monarchs – and it was at Hampton Court that he died in 1707.

Even when she was staying at Windsor Castle, Queen Anne used to come over to Hampton Court to preside over meetings of the Privy Council, which were held in the Cartoon Gallery. She had various work done outside as well as inside the Palace. The little low hedges of box which had bordered the flower-beds of the Great Fountain Garden were now uprooted, for the Queen disliked the smell; turf and gravel were laid down instead. The Lion Gates were set up and the Diana Fountain restored. She had the Chapel refurbished – the old Holyday Closets were largely demolished and transformed into a Royal Pew, and a new organ by Christopher Shrider was installed at a cost of £800.

The Queen granted Wren the tenancy of a pleasant house by the Palace gates. However she did not always pay the craftsmen their bills, especially when they were for work done in King William's time. So Jean Tijou, who claimed he was owed no less than £1,889. 1s. $6\frac{1}{4}d.$, was told shortly "There is no money at present for arrears".

149

Meanwhile Anne kept, according to Jonathan Swift, "the best table in England", which cost her £1,000 a month. She came to Hampton Court twice a week "for the air", and when her legs grew too gouty to carry her about, she rode across the parks in a one-horse chaise, chasing stags.

It was an incident at Hampton Court which inspired Alexander Pope's satirical poem *The Rape of the Lock*.*

The charming Arabella Fermor, referred to in the poem as Belinda, was sipping coffee at the Palace, after a game of ombre, when a gallant by the name of Lord Petre ("the Baron") came up behind her and snipped off a lock of her hair. The young lady was horrified,

> "For ever cursed be this detested day,
> Which snatch'd my best, my favourite curl away!
> Happy! ah ten times happy had I been
> If Hampton Court these eyes had never seen!"

Lord Petre refused to return the lock and a quarrel ensued between the two families.

Despite the frothy artificiality of the diction, which Pope used deliberately to point the triviality of the dispute, the poem gives a vivid impression of Palace life in the reign of Queen Anne,

> "Hither the heroes and the nymphs resort,
> To taste awhile the pleasures of a court;
> In various talk the instructive hours they pass'd
> Who gave the ball, or paid the visit last;
> One speaks the glory of the British Queen,
> And one describes a charming Indian screen;
> A third interprets motions, looks, and eyes;
> At every word a reputation dies."

On 4th May 1710 the Queen entertained some oriental gentlemen referred to as "Indian kings", and in October 1711 ambassadors from France came to Hampton Court. Jonathan Swift noted in his *Journal to Stella* (3rd November 1711) how she had travelled there on a day of "terrible rain", and how he had also hoped to stay; "I stuffed the Secretary's† pockets with papers, which he must read and settle at Hampton Court, where he went today,

---

* The shorter, two-canto version of the poem was published in 1712, and the fuller, five-canto version in 1714
† Henry St John, Viscount Bolingbroke

and stays some time. They have no lodgings for me there, so I can't go, for the town is small, chargeable, and inconvenient.''

The Queen's health was deteriorating, and in the absence of any obvious heir apart from over fifty Stuart claimants (some at least of whom might have been persuaded to turn Anglican), she eventually agreed that the crown should pass to the Electors of Hanover. Their claim was through the female line only; Charles I's sister Elizabeth had married the Elector Palatine of Bohemia, and her fourth child Sophia had married Ernest Augustus, Elector of Hanover. The eldest child of this union was George Lewis. It was decided that the crown should go first to Sophia, a witty, lively old lady in her eighties, and then to her heirs.

Anne was difficult to persuade, for she did not like German George and considered the Old Pretender's claim much stronger; but the latter would give no assurance that he would maintain freedom of religious observance, and had allied himself so firmly to the French that there was a fear of civil war in the event of his succession. Reluctantly therefore she agreed. Although only in her late forties, she had fallen prematurely into dotage. Rumours of her death circulated some time before it actually happened at Kensington on 1st August 1714. The usual desperate remedies had been tried, including shaving her head and blistering her with hot irons. She finally died in the early hours of that morning. Dr Arbuthnot wrote to Swift: ''I believe sleep was never more welcome to a weary traveller than death was to her.'' The Electress Sophia had narrowly missed becoming Queen of Great Britain, dying only two months before Anne's last illness, and the accession of George was stage-managed to take place as smoothly and quickly as possible.

King George I, however, was in no particular hurry. He never cared greatly for England, nor did much to improve his English. Every two years or so of his reign he used to make quite a lengthy visit to Hanover. He inherited much of his father's phlegm, and little of his mother's wit. A stolid, obstinate, unimaginative man, he could be particularly sadistic in his treatment of his nearest relations. His own wife, Sophia Dorothea, he shut away in the castle of Ahlden because of her alleged affair with Count

151

The Cartoon Gallery
Built to house the Raphael Cartoons, was used by Queen Anne as a council chamber. Tapestries from Raphael's designs now hang on the walls instead of the original drawings. Below are paintings of the life and times of Henry VIII, including on the extreme left, the ''Field of the Cloth of Gold''.

(*Opposite, top*) The south front from the Pond Garden
On the left is part of Wolsey's palace and on the right can be seen the taller mass of the south front of the palace designed by Wren. The Pond Garden was originally laid out in the 16th century for Henry VIII.

(*Opposite, below*) Palace from across the Thames
This is the view of the south side of the Palace seen from the bank of what is known as Cigarette Island.

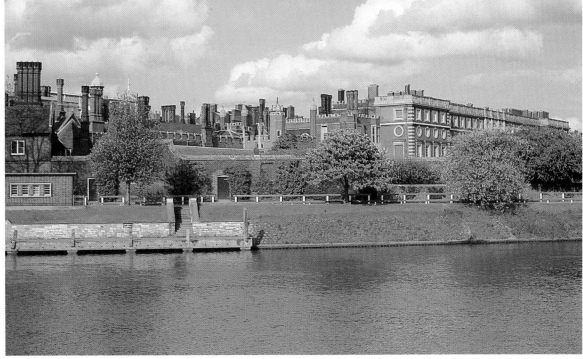

(*Above*) The Orangery seen from the Knot Garden
The Orangery, built for William and Mary, now houses Mantegna's paintings of the "Triumph of Caesar." The Knot Garden is relatively modern, but this was the favourite form of garden in Tudor times.

(*Opposite, top left*) The South Front from the South-East

(*Opposite, top right*) Fountain Court
Designed by Sir Christopher Wren for William and Mary. One of the walls collapsed while it was being built, killing three or four men.

(*Opposite*) The Banqueting House
Wren designed this to provide William III with a semi-informal riverside dining room.

The Queen's Gallery
A spacious room of the 'Queen's Side' of the Palace, completed for Queen Anne. The marble
fireplace is by John Nost, and the set of tulip vases were made in Delft for William III.

(*Opposite, top*) Laburnum Walk
Situated near the north wall of the Palace grounds, the laburnum walk is
one of the glories of Hampton Court gardens in May.

(*Opposite, left*) The Tudor Tennis Court
This was built for Henry VIII in 1529-30. In his youth the King was athletic
and a keen player of Royal, or Real, Tennis.

(*Opposite, right*) The Great Vine
This Black Hamburgh vine was planted in 1769 and still yields a copious
harvest of grapes.

Königsmark (Königsmark himself disappeared and was probably murdered at George's instigation). He left her imprisoned there until she died thirty-two years later.

Therefore when he arrived as king on 18th September 1714, he was without a queen. In his train came his two German mistresses. Their names were Fräulein Schulenberg and Frau Kielmansegge, and it was almost universally agreed that they were rapacious, stupid and excessively ugly ladies. Fräulein Schulenberg, of whom Lady Mary Wortley Montagu remarked, "She was duller than the King, and consequently did not find out that he was so", was very tall and skinny, so she was nicknamed "The Maypole". As for Frau Kielmansegge, she was almost universally disliked. The King's daughter-in-law, Princess Caroline of Anspach, thought her a wicked, scheming woman who "never stuck a pin in her gown without design". She was younger and perhaps a little livelier than Fräulein Schulenberg, but revoltingly fat. Horace Walpole described her thus, "Two fierce black eyes, large and rolling, beneath which two lofty arched eyebrows. Two acres of cheeks spread with crimson, an ocean of neck that overflowed and was not distinguished from the lower part of her body, and no part restrained by stays." She became known as "The Elephant and Castle".

These two ladies, being not only unattractive but also foreign, did not endear themselves to the people at large, nor did they do anything to render George more popular. "Good pipple, why you abuse us?" Fräulein Schulenberg is reputed to have said, leaning out of her sedan chair, "We are come for all your goods?" "Yes, damn ye!" was the reply, "and for our chattels too."*

It was not even as if they added any excitement or titillation to relieve the tedium of George's very dull Court. He installed them at Hampton Court Palace, and there they would sit with the King for hours, cutting figures out of paper while he puffed his pipe contentedly and applauded when he thought the silhouettes resembled some notable person of the day. It was possibly after them that Frog (or Vrouw) Walk, on the west side by the Palace gate, is named, "Frog" being a corruption of "Frau".

* From Horace Walpole's *Reminiscences*. The anecdote has some justification, for they appropriated the late Queen's jewels.

A king who is said to have exclaimed in his German accent, "I hate all boets and bainters!" was unlikely to be a great patron of the arts. He failed to appreciate Sir Christopher Wren, who in 1718 was dismissed from his office as Surveyor-General, and was succeeded by William Benson, a man of very little account. Wren, by then in his eighties, was asked to answer accusations of mismanagement. He wrote sadly from his house at Hampton Court, "as I am dismissed, having worn out (by God's mercy) a long life in the Royal service, and having made some figure in the world, I hope it will be allow'd me to die in peace.*

A limited amount of patronage was extended to Sir James Thornhill (1675/6–1734) who had succeeded Verrio as a painter of large-scale decorative compositions. Thornhill's greatest work was the Painted Hall at Greenwich Hospital, which took him nineteen years to complete. His work is now generally preferred to Verrio's, but he was not quite as well paid. At Hampton Court he was commissioned to paint the ceiling of the Queen's Bedroom, for the use of the Prince and Princess of Wales (George II and Caroline of Anspach), and for this he was paid £3. 11s. per yard, or £457. 10s. for the whole work. The central design shows Aurora, goddess of the dawn, rising from the sea in her golden chariot. In the coved cornice which frames it Thornhill painted portraits of the royal family: George I, the Prince and Princess of Wales, and their son Frederick, then aged nine.

Despite this portrayal of family unity, George I heartily disliked his daughter-in-law and for most of his reign was not on speaking terms with his son. But to begin with, all was reasonably civil, and the young couple enjoyed themselves at Hampton Court. Surrounded by a much more cheerful entourage than the Hanoverians provided at their father's court, they boated on the Thames, played cards or bowls, or strolled in the gardens – the Prince sometimes escaping from the charms of his quite voluptuous wife to flirt with her ladies-in-waiting, Mary Bellenden and Molly Lepell.

The quarrel began with an incident at the christening of the Prince's second son (the Duke of Cumberland) when the King insisted on the Duke of Newcastle being one of the godparents.

---

* He died in his other house, in St James's Street, in 1723 at the age of 91, and was buried in St Paul's Cathedral.

The Prince, who loathed the Duke, expostulated to him, "Rascal, I shall find you out!" meaning that he would get his own back. Newcastle thought he had said "fight" instead of "find" and complained to the King that his life had been threatened. King George then banished the Prince and Princess to a separate court, and deprived them of their children, for whose education he assumed responsibility himself. So when George I was at St James's they were at Leicester House, and when he was at Hampton Court they had a separate establishment at Richmond.

"It was strange he could not eat without being stared at," the Czar Peter the Great had remarked when he visited William III in 1698. But the practice of dining in public had long been established among British monarchs, and it was continued by the Hanoverians. The Public Dining Room at Hampton Court was begun as a Music Room for the Prince and Princess of Wales (music was one of the few arts encouraged by George I, particularly because of Handel's coming to England), and the Audit Office Declared Accounts for 1718 show that the decoration of the room was finished by then; they include:

"Painting and flooring the Musick room.
Grinling Gibbons for carved work in the Musick Room.
David Lance for plastering in the Musick room . . .
Thomas Highmore for painting the said rooms.
Benjamin Jackson for white and veined Marble, Egyptian marble fire hearths, coving stones and workmanship in the Musick room etc."*

On the whole the Court of George I was a pretty dull affair, but it was enlivened occasionally by the performance of plays. In September – October 1718 seven were performed in the Great Hall. These included *Hamlet, Henry VIII, or the Fall of Wolsey*, and Ben Jonson's *Volpone*, and they were performed by the King's Company of Actors among whom were Colley Cibber and Mrs Oldfield. The actors were more used to playing in Drury Lane and were rather ill at ease having to perform in front of the King and nobility. However, as Sir Richard Steele remarked afterwards, George was so delighted with them that he "was not

* It has been maintained by Ernest Law and others that this room was redecorated by William Kent in 1732, but as Gerald Heath has pointed out, there seems to be little evidence to support this. The fireplace with the Hanoverian coat-of-arms could refer equally well to George I or George II.

sure the King would not keep them to fill the posts at Court that he saw them so fit for in the play.''

These plays seem to have been performed in the Hall as it stood, but in the following year work started on fitting up a theatre inside it. Sir James Thornhill was commissioned to design scenery for it; carpenters, painters and even a bricklayer were employed, and there were windows of glass. The theatre within the Great Hall seems to have survived until about 1790.

George left for his last visit to Hanover on 3rd June 1727, together with his Turkish servant Mustapha and the Duchess of Kendal (Fräulein Schulenberg). When they landed in Holland George celebrated by devouring a huge banquet including a great number of melons. The next day he set off by coach towards Hanover, but was taken violently ill. Whether he was upset by the melons, or by the shock of reading a letter from his wife who had recently died in her castle prison, he himself died of apoplexy shortly afterwards.

When he was told of his accession, the new king was at Richmond and, having retired to bed for the afternoon, was just in the act of doing up his breeches. This was not really in character. When he had been Prince of Wales he had not been given much responsibility, and was not even made regent during his father's regular visits to Hanover. But once he came to the throne George II proved himself very much his father's son, equally stolid and irascible, preferring Hanover and detesting England, and so predictable it was said one could set one's clock by him. From 1728 to 1738 he spent two months of every summer at Hampton Court, but the court he kept there was insufferably dull. "No mill-horse ever went in a more constant track," wrote Lord Hervey from the Palace on 21st July 1733, ". . . Walking, chaises, levees and audiences fill the morning; at night the King plays at commerce and backgammon, and the Queen at quadrille." The King had a mistress, a pleasant, rather intelligent woman called Mrs Henrietta Howard, and while she was in favour he would visit her in her rooms at the Palace every evening at nine o'clock precisely. On Wednesdays and Saturdays he went stag-hunting (fox-hunting he despised), joined by his daughter Princess Amelia, who was very keen on horses, and sometimes – reluctantly – by Mrs Howard. "We hunt with great noise and violence", she remarked, "and have every day a considerable chance to have a neck broke."

The King and Queen both ate hugely. The menu which greeted them on 10th June 1731, when they, the Prince and Princess of Wales, their younger son the Duke of Cumberland and their suite had just arrived at the Palace from Richmond and Kew, was however graded more according to rank than to appetite. For their majesties, dinner included vermicelli soup, chickens with peas and lettuce, a fricassee of veal, patties of various sorts, mutton cutlets, roast beef and beef hash, artichokes, ragout, "cream brulée", roast hare, pheasants and blackbirds. Gravy to accompany this feast was made from beef, mutton and veal. For their supper they had broiled shoulder of mutton, chicken with butter and parsley, pheasants, salmon, buttered eggs with cheese, peas and lettuce, anchovy salad, gooseberry fool and roast quails. The Prince and Princess of Wales were allowed almost as much, and their menu included lobsters – probably quite a rarity at inland Hampton Court. The little Duke was provided with a more childish repast – roast beef, cherry tarts, baked custards and a pudding. The Prince of Wales's pages dined pretty well on beans and bacon, fricassee of chicken, roast beef and goose. Meanwhile poor Mrs Howard was allowed no more than mutton and cabbage.

At Hampton Court the King had various work done about the Palace. The Queen's Presence and Guard Chambers were completed, the Queen's Staircase decorated, and the apartments along the south side of Fountain Court were made into small informal rooms for the personal use of the royal family. In one of these is King George II's field-bed, a collapsible one used by the King on campaign; the mattress is covered in white kid. Queen Caroline's state bed dates from about 1729; its crimson silk damask is glued on to an elaborate structure of carved deal.

At the south-east corner of the Palace a rather plain suite of apartments was provided for the Prince of Wales. Far more care

A Perspective View of the ROYAL PALACE *at* HAMPTON COURT.

and craftsmanship, however, seem to have been lavished on the suite provided for the Duke of Cumberland. Part of the east side of Clock Court, still Tudor, was rebuilt by William Kent in a very early example of the neo-Gothic style. The rooms have a certain charm, despite their incongruity. Completed in 1732, they were the last part of the Palace to be built.

Meanwhile the gardens were simplified and expanses of green lawn replaced the earlier scrollwork. Running parallel to Broad Walk were planted a row of yew trees, severely clipped according to the fashion favoured by Kent and encouraged by the Queen. Alexander Pope, however, thought them gloomy and

A Perspective View of the Royal Palace at Hampton Court. This engraving dating from about 1770 shows the lines of pyramid-shaped yew trees so criticised by Alexander Pope.

163

Queen Caroline of Anspach
Wife of George II, by Joseph Highmore

called them "pyramids of dark green, continually repeated, not unlike a funeral procession".

Queen Caroline of Anspach was much more affable, articulate and enlightened than her husband, and when he was away in Hanover it was noticeable that the Court became quite cheerful and lively. She kept on good terms with the chief minister, Robert Walpole, and between the two of them did much to influence the King in matters of state. Unlike the King, she took an interest in literature, the arts and theology. She was not, however, particularly observant in her prayers.

Among the private rooms at the Palace fitted up for her was a small chapel with a pretty domed ceiling. Here was installed her private chaplain Dr Maddox. The adjoining room was the Queen's Bathing Closet. Here she was washed and dressed, attended (until she resigned her office as lady of the bedchamber) by Mrs Howard. The Queen insisted on Mrs Howard going down on her knees while she held the basin and ewer for the Queen to wash her hands. Meanwhile the chaplain continued with his prayers and the door between the rooms was left ajar. But Dr Maddox was shocked to see a picture of a nude Venus over the fireplace. "And a very proper altarpiece is here, Madam!" he expostulated. Crossly the Queen ordered the door to be shut. Immediately the chaplain stopped his prayers, and when she asked him why, replied, "I refuse to whistle the word of God through a keyhole."

Lord Hervey improved on the incident by writing a short skit in his *Memoirs*. Caroline is shown at her toilet*, attended by ladies of the Court; at the same time a litany is being intoned next door. "I pray, my good Lady Sundon," the Queen is made to say, "shut a little that door; these creatures pray so loud, one cannot hear oneself speak." (Lady Sundon goes to shut the door.) "So, so, not quite so much; leave it enough open for those parsons to think we may hear, and enough shut that we may not hear quite so much."

Caroline shared with her husband an extraordinary loathing

---

* There is a traditional nursery rhyme which goes:
> "Queenie, Queenie Caroline
> Washed her head in turpentine,
> Turpentine to make it shine,
> Queenie, Queenie Caroline."

Apparently turpentine was used to kill off the nits in one's hair. Caroline was a progressive woman in some ways, and had her daughters Amelia and Caroline inoculated against smallpox.

for their eldest son, vastly preferring the younger, William Duke of Cumberland.* It is difficult to understand why. Admittedly Frederick Prince of Wales was irresponsible and something of a gambler, but he seems to have been a lively little man of great charm. He was quite accomplished; he wrote poetry in both English and French, and played the viola da gamba well enough to give private concerts. He also enjoyed cricket and boating, and he was no more dissolute than was fashionable. But the Hanoverian kings never managed to get on, one generation with another; George II called his son a puppy and a changeling. And it is surprising how vituperative Caroline was: "My dear first-born is the greatest ass, and the greatest liar, and the greatest canaille, and the greatest beast, in the whole world, and I most heartily wish he was out of it."

Frederick married Princess Augusta of Saxe-Gotha, a pleasant girl, rather quiet and extremely polite. The King and Queen approved, although George would not let the young couple go on any progresses, nor dine in public; no doubt he was afraid that Frederick's popularity would be increased even more. "Popularity", the Queen declared, "makes me sick, but Fritz's popularity makes me vomit." The King then departed on one of his regular trips to Hanover, largely to visit his new mistress Madame Walmoden.

The following summer (1737) the royal family were all at Hampton Court, and it began to be rumoured that Princess Augusta was pregnant. The Queen could hardly believe it – she probably thought Frederick was impotent – and she had no wish to believe it either, for if it were a boy, it would lessen her younger son's chances of ever succeeding to the throne. She questioned Augusta very closely as to when the baby might be due, the Princess replied evasively. The King and Queen were anxious that the birth should take place at Hampton Court, since they wanted to witness the event (there must be no tales of warming-pan babies this time); Frederick was equally determined that it should take place in London. The Princess had not apparently grown very large with this pregnancy, and it was generally supposed that she would not give birth until the autumn.

166

* Later to be known as the "Butcher", after the massacre of Culloden.

The Music Party
By Philippe Mercier *c.* 1753. Frederick, Prince of Wales, is shown with his three eldest sisters, performing in the setting of the Banqueting House at Hampton Court. The painting itself is at Windsor.

The Queen's Staircase
This was not decorated until
the time of George II. The large
painting by Honthorst on the
right, however, is 17th
century, and shows the Duke
of Buckingham (disguised as
Mercury) introducing the
Liberal Arts to Charles I and
Henrietta Maria (disguised as
Apollo and Diana).

On 31st July 1737 the Princess dined with the King and Queen
in the Public Dining Room; the Prince did not come, since he
was not on speaking terms with the King. After the meal Augusta
went to rejoin her husband in his apartments (still known as the
Prince of Wales's rooms). Then her labour-pains started. Frederick insisted that they should travel immediately to St James's
so that the baby should be born there. Despite all her protests,
the Princess was bundled downstairs – no doubt via the Prince
of Wales's staircase, the most surreptitious way out – and into
a coach. With them came two of the Prince's valets, Mr Bloodworth and Mr Vreid, (the latter was reputed to be a surgeon and
man-midwife), Lady Archibald Hamilton (the Prince's mistress),
and Mrs Clavering and Mrs Paine (two of the Princess's
ladies-in-waiting).

The Princess pleaded to be allowed to stay at Hampton Court, but her husband was adamant. "Courage! Courage! ah, quelle sottise!" he said, and assured her that it would all "be over in a minute". So poor Augusta, howling and pinching her attendants in her agony, was conveyed to St James's Palace, arriving there at about ten o'clock. The Prince ordered that all lights should be put out, so that no one could see what was happening. Nothing had been prepared, any more than it would have been at Hampton Court. There were no sheets to be found, so the accouchement took place between two table-cloths. Three-quarters of an hour after their arrival, the Princess gave birth to "a little rat of a girl, about the bigness of a good large toothpick case".*

Meanwhile the King and Queen were completely unaware of what was happening. After their meal they had gone off, the King downstairs, and the Queen upstairs, to play their separate games of cards, and went to bed at eleven as usual.

As soon as the baby was born, the Prince sent a servant to Hampton Court with the message that the Princess was in labour; he arrived at about half-past one. The Queen was woken up by Lady Tichburne (one of her ladies-in-waiting), and at first she thought the Palace was on fire. When she was told what the matter was she exclaimed, "My God, my nightgown! I'll go to her this moment." "Your nightgown, madam, and your coaches too;" said Lady Tichburne, "the Princess is at St James's!"

The Queen was incredulous and the King irate, expostulating to her in German, "This is all your fault. There is a false child will be put upon you, and how will you answer it to all your children?" Caroline dressed and ordered coaches to be got ready. Then she, with her two elder daughters, their ladies-in-waiting, and three courtiers, set off for St James's, arriving there at about four o'clock.

She went straight to the Princess, and said to her,

"Apparement, madame, vous avez horriblement souffert."

"Point de tout," answered Augusta, "Ce n'est rien."

Since the child was a girl, and a puny one at that, the Queen came to the conclusion after all that it was genuinely Frederick's

169

---

* Hervey's *Memoirs*. The "little rat" grew up into an attractive young woman and married the Duke of Brunswick.

and Augusta's child. Had it been a bouncing boy, then her suspicions really would have been aroused. But she was furious with her son. "I hope in God," she declared at breakfast, back at Hampton Court, "that I shall never see that monster's face again." The King was even more outraged and, once the christening was over, ordered him out of St James's. "Thank God," he said, "tomorrow night the puppy will be out of my house." The Prince's household moved to Kew, as soon as the Princess was well enough. Meanwhile the King and Queen stayed on at Hampton Court until 28th October.

Caroline never did see her son again. She had concealed it from everybody but the King, but she was suffering from an umbilical rupture. She became violently ill on 8th November and after great agonies died eleven days later.

CHAPTER ELEVEN

The Neglected Palace

"What a beautiful place! What a real palace! How can anyone leave Hampton Court and live in the Pavilion?"
Mary Russell Mitford, 1782–1855
(July 5th 1822)

All this time the only way to cross the Thames at Hampton Court had been by ferry or private boat. There is a painting of the Palace dating from about 1640 which shows a flat-bottomed ferry plying its trade between the Surrey and Middlesex banks, and capable of transporting, however precariously, a horse and carriage. It is reproduced on page 118.

The first bridge across the river at this point was built in the mid-eighteenth century. It was designed by Samuel Stevens and Benjamin Ludgater, and owned by Mr James Clarke, Squire of the Manor of East Molesey. The bridge was opened on 15th December 1753. It was a curiously Chinese affair, constructed of wood and consisting of seven hump-backed arches with little pavilions at each intersection. It is hard to see how it can ever have been used for anything more than pedestrian traffic.

The bridge was replaced in 1778 by one which was rather more substantial, though still made of wood, and this lasted until 1865. The Crown did not take up the option of paying for its construction, consequently this bridge, like the earlier one, belonged to James Clarke. Clarke and his successors exacted heavy tolls from those who used it: a halfpenny or a penny for pedestrians, a shilling for a single-horse carriage or cab, and for a coach drawn by six horses, two shillings and sixpence.

The reason why the Crown decided not to finance the bridge was probably the King's lack of interest in the Palace. After the death of Queen Caroline, George II used it only for occasional visits and seldom spent even a night there. With his new mistress Lady Yarmouth* and a few coach-loads of attendants, he would

171

---

* When Caroline knew she was dying she begged him to take another wife. The distraught George replied tearfully, no, he would have mistresses instead. That was no impediment to marriage, observed the Queen. It never had been; however George did not re-marry and did indeed take mistresses.

A View of the Bridge over the Thames at Hampton Court

The First Bridge over the Thames at Hampton Court. This pretty but unpractical bridge was opened in 1753. The view in this contemporary engraving is downstream, and part of the Palace may be seen on the left.

arrive at midday on summer Saturdays, dine, walk about the gardens for an hour, and then depart again.

Always cantankerous, George's temper did not improve with age, and when he was really annoyed he would kick his hat about the room. Prince Frederick, who all his life seems to have been his father's particular *bête noire*, died suddenly in 1751. King George put on a great show of grief and paid a personal visit to Princess Augusta and her children – he even managed to shed

The Queen's Drawing-room
After the death of William III, some of the
Queen's rooms were completed for Queen Anne.
The Drawing Room was decorated by Antonio
Verrio and this wall shows Anne's husband
George of Denmark riding naked on the back of
a dolphin.

Ceiling of Queen's Bedroom
The ceiling was painted by Sir James Thornhill,
the central panel showing Aurora, the goddess of
the dawn, is framed with portraits of the family
of George I: his son (later George II) and
daughter-in-law and their son Frederick (here
aged 9).

(*Opposite*) The King's Staircase
Created for William III, this was the ceremonial entrance to the King's State-Rooms. The wrought-iron balustrade was designed by Jean Tijou and the wall and ceiling paintings by Antonio Verrio celebrate in allegory the prosperity looked for under the reign of the House of Orange.

(*Left*)
Ceiling of the King's Bedroom
This was designed by Antonio Verrio for William III. It shows the shepherd Endymion asleep in the arms of Morpheus the god of sleep and dreaming, no doubt, of Diana the goddess of the moon and of chastity.

(*below*) George II's Private Chamber
This is the only room in the Palace with its original wallpaper, dating from the 18th century. The oriental porcelain on the overmantel was part of Mary II's fabulous collection; in the foreground is a velvet-topped gaming table and the large portrait on the right is a posthumous one of Lady Venetia Digby, painted by Van Dyck.

tears. Popular opinion concerning the Prince was summed up in the anonymous epitaph,

> "Here lies Fred
> Who was alive and is dead;
> Had it been his father,
> I had much rather;
> Had it been his brother,
> Still better than another;
> Had it been his sister,
> No one would have missed her;
> Had it been the whole generation,
> Still better for the nation;
> But since 'tis only Fred
> Who was alive and is dead,
> There's no more to be said."

After Frederick's death George II seems to have transferred some of his dislike to his eldest son (later George III) – it is extraordinary the hatred Hanoverian monarchs habitually bore for their heirs. On one occasion when he was at Hampton Court, he is said to have boxed the boy's ears so viciously that he put him off the Palace for life. Young George, as soon as he reached his legal majority in 1755, refused to pay any further attention to the dictates of his grandfather and declared he would do exactly as he pleased. The old King sent for the boy to reprimand him. The Prince (according to Waldegrave) was "flustered and sulky; bowed, but scarce made any answer; so the conference ended very little to the satisfaction of either party."

George III came to the throne on 25th October 1760. His accession was greeted with a sense of relief. Horace Walpole described the twenty-two-year-old King thus,
"His person is tall and full of dignity, his countenance florid and good natured, his manner graceful and obliging ... The Sovereign does not stand in one spot with his eyes fixed on the ground, and dropping bits of German news. He walks about and speaks freely to everybody."

Hampton Court Palace, however, had unfortunate associations

The Knot Garden.
A replica of the Tudor type of garden where the plot was divided into geometrical shapes and the beds edged with low-growing shrubs such as box and lavender and flowers or herbs planted in between.

177

for him, and he refused to use it, preferring Windsor Castle, and also Buckingham House (the nucleus of Buckingham Palace), which was acquired for his wife Queen Charlotte* in 1762. So at Hampton Court the state-rooms were immediately shut up, the furniture removed, and even the kitchen equipment sent to London so that it could be used for the coronation. In 1766 the Raphael Cartoons were taken out and hung first in Buckingham House, and then, in 1788, at Windsor Castle, where they remained until they were returned to the Palace in 1808.

At Hampton Court a certain amount of maintenance work was done. Wolsey's old gatehouse was in a poor state; unfortunately instead of repairing the original structure, it was partly demolished and then rebuilt, losing its top two storeys in the process.

The gardens fared better. They were in the care of Lancelot Brown, known as 'Capability' Brown on account of his characteristic remark "I see great capability of improvement here." Fortunately at Hampton Court he did not undertake any drastic remodelling of the grounds, but preserved them very much as they were. It was during his term of office (in 1796) that the Black Hamburgh vine was planted which is now known as the Great Vine and still bears a copious harvest of grapes. The vine is said to have been a cutting from one at a house called Valentines in Ilford, Essex in 1758. The Hampton Court vine grew to a tremendous size, possibly because of its proximity to the river-bed. By 1892 it was reported† as having a stem 38 inches in circumference and principal branches 110 feet long, and giving an average yearly yield of about 2,000 bunches of grapes. Today the branches are kept to about the same length but the girth of the stem has approximately doubled.

Hampton Court Palace had even during the reign of George II become far more of a show-place than a royal residence. A housekeeper was installed and she was naturally a woman of great influence. Once the Court was removed a large number of the building's approximately 1,100 rooms lay empty. A few servants and officials still lived there legitimately, and probably there were also hangers-on who had bribed their way into acquir-

---

* Queen Charlotte's Bed, now at Hampton Court, was never used at this place but at Windsor. Together with its suite of chairs and stools, it was designed by Robert Adam, and is said to have cost the phenomenal sum of £14,000 – the equivalent of nearly £1 million of present currency.

† *Farm, Field and Fireside*, 1st January 1892. See also page 196.

ing accommodation; no doubt the housekeeper did extremely well out of this.

It was decided to put the whole matter under the control of the Lord Chamberlain. Apartments, about forty in number, were allotted by "grace and favour" 'to recipients considered deserving. They were mostly slightly impoverished members of the aristocracy, or people of some position in public life, together with their female dependants. No rooms at Hampton Court were to be tenanted without a warrant, or written authorization from the Lord Chamberlain addressed to the housekeeper. One applicant was Dr Samuel Johnson; it is a pity he was not successful. Inevitably there were abuses of the system – some of the official tenants did not use their apartments and lent them or let them out to others "for motives far less pure than those of Friendship or Acquaintance" – so wrote the Lord Chamberlain to the Under-Housekeeper (20th July 1780) in an attempt to put an end to such irregularities.

One of the early Grace and Favour residents was Thomas Bradshaw, who had been private secretary to the Duke of Grafton – a very confidential secretary indeed who had helped the Duke in his amorous adventures and been rewarded with a pension of £1,500 per annum. The Duke also obtained for him in about 1770 a magnificent suite at Hampton Court, consisting of sixty or seventy rooms. Here he could live like a lord. However Bradshaw squandered all his money at a prodigious rate and, in the autumn of 1774, took a gun and shot himself.

Another suicide, or probable suicide, among the Grace and Favour residents was Richard Tickell, brother-in-law of the dramatist Sheridan. Tickell may have been depressed by debts or political concerns, or just possibly his death may have been an accident. His rooms were on the top storey of the South Front, and outside there is a ledge over the capitals of the pillars. Apparently it was Tickell's habit to climb out of the window onto this ledge to sit and read, surrounded by flower-pots. On 4th November 1793, when he was just about to leave Hampton Court to spend the winter in London, his wife discovered his body lying on the path, sixty feet below the parapet. Whether he had overbalanced or jumped to his death, his fall was so violent that his head made a hole one foot deep in the gravel.

From 1795 until 1802 a suite of rooms was occupied by the exiled Stadtholder William V of Orange, his native Holland having been invaded by the French. He lived in some dignity with his family and servants in apartments on the east side of Clock Court, and two of the state rooms (the Queen's Guard and Presence Chambers) were opened up for his use. He was a corpulent gentleman, a cousin of the reigning King in that they were both grandsons of George II; George III came on occasion to visit him in his rooms during the eight years he spent at Hampton Court.

At this time the tolls for crossing Hampton Court Bridge were collected by a man called Feltham, and there was a gate to prevent anyone crossing without paying. The King was hunting on the north side of the river when the deer broke away and swam over to the Surrey bank. The hounds jumped the gate, and then came a number of huntsmen shouting "The King!" Feltham opened the gate and let them through without paying. Then another larger group came up, again shouting "The King!" This time Feltham stood firm. "Hang me," he said, "if I open my gate again until I see your money. I pay £400 a year for this bridge, and I laid out £1,000 upon it. I've let King George through, God bless him! I know of no other king in England. If you have brought the King of France, hang me if I let him through without the blunt!"

Then Feltham recognized King George himself among the party. With a bow, he let him and all the others cross over to Molesey where the hunt was in full cry. Later the King sent back to ask why they had been held up at the bridge. He was told about the toll-keeper and that it was customary for a guinea to be paid whenever the Royal Hunt passed over. The incident amused him and he decided to give Feltham considerably more than that fee. The next time King George crossed the bridge, on the way back from visiting the Stadtholder William, he pulled down the window of the coach and called to Feltham, "No fear of the King of France coming today!"

By the end of George III's reign the Palace was becoming noticeably decayed, and since the Prince Regent took very little interest in it, being far more occupied with the building of the Royal Pavilion at Brighton, even basic repair-work was neglected. Almost the only positive improvement done at this time was the removal of the theatre which was still cluttering up the Great Hall. This was effected under the surveyorship of Sir James Wyatt in about 1798. In the preceding years there had been some repairs to the glass, joists, gutters and brickwork; and it is with relief that the author of an article in the *Gentleman's Magazine* (March 1812) notes "the time-serving theatre erected in the late reign, taking up so much of the interior of the Hall, is done away". Then in 1830–31 the parishioners of St Mary's Hampton were allowed to use the Great Hall for services while their new church was being built.

Vistors to the Palace were shown around, no doubt rather summarily, by the housekeeper or her assistant, at a fee of about a shilling a head. Oddly enough they were still not always shown the Great Hall; this was like a performance of *Hamlet* without the principal character, a contemporary commented.* Mary Russell Mitford was most enthusiastic. The visitors were, however, shown (according to the memoirs of Hannah More) "an ordinary room, full of original furniture of the Cardinal, chiefly curious for its antiquity, consisting only of cane tables, chairs etc." There was also an old shoe which was reputed to have belonged to Wolsey; but it is very doubtful whether any of these relics were genuine. Sir Walter Scott took a tour round the Palace when he came to visit his son there in April 1828; he remarked, "The pictures are not very excellent, but they are curious, which is as interesting to conoisseurs." He came again a month later in company with Tom Moore, Samuel Rogers, William Wordsworth and his wife and daughter, but they seem to have contented themselves with strolling happily around the gardens.

The Duke of Wellington too was a frequent visitor to the Palace. His mother the Countess of Mornington was one of the Grace and Favour ladies and lived here for about thirty years. She had apartments on the east side of the building, next to the walled garden that lies behind Broad Walk on the way to the

181

* *The Mirror of Literature, Amusement and Instruction*, 14th March 1835

Tudor Tennis Court*. She loved to sit out here, and it is still known as Lady Mornington's Garden. Another favourite sitting-out place, where the old ladies used to congregate to gossip, was an alcove at the north end of the East Front – the Duke christened this "Purr Corner".

A royal stud had existed at Hampton Court since the time of William III, and the Prince Regent took particular delight in it. When he ascended the throne as George IV, he decided to improve the stabling and to extend the paddocks. There were forty-three paddocks, of three to five acres each, in Bushey and Home Parks, and the King kept thirty-three brood mares and many famous stallions. The stud continued to flourish in the time of William IV, but at his death all the horses were sold, at a total figure of 15,692 guineas, and the paddocks were leased out until Queen Victoria re-started the stud in 1851.

Although visitors to the Palace were still conducted around in a brisk and summary way by one of the housekeeper's assistants, William IV decided that they ought to have more to see for their shilling's worth; so he had a great many pictures brought from the other royal residences (Windsor Castle, St James's, Kensington, Buckingham House and Carlton House) to adorn the walls – but apparently with more regard to quantity than to quality. He did something to repair the fabric and decoration of the building. The King's Staircase and the Banqueting House were restored, and the latter was made into a private apartment. The old Astronomical Clock was in a bad state. A letter from B. L. Vulliamy to the Board of Works reported, "The Great Clock at Hampton Court has gone until it will go no longer for want of cleaning", and he offered to do the job for £200. Restoration was postponed, however, and the clock was taken out in 1835. Vulliamy installed a new clock which had come from St James's, but the movement was not powerful enough to drive the Astronomical Clock as well. The old clock in pieces was stored in an out-house, and here the dials were discovered in 1879. The clock was finally restored by James Thwaites and a new movement made for it by the following year.

The one part of the Palace which was still used for its original

* Before Wren's rebuilding, this was the site of the Queen's Gallery designed for Anne Boleyn.

purpose was the Chapel, and here the Grace and Favour residents would come to pray on Sundays. One of them was a Sir Horace Seymour, a particularly handsome fellow and hero of Waterloo; he was moreover a widower and therefore eligible. It was always the tradition that the gentlemen sat one side of the Chapel Royal and the ladies the other. One Sunday in the summer of 1831 a young lady fainted during the service. Sir Horace walked across, picked her up in his arms, carried her to his apartments and left her in the care of his housekeeper, while he himself returned to the Chapel. The next Sunday another young lady fainted, and Sir Horace came to her aid the same way. The third Sunday the whole pattern was again repeated.

After that Sir Horace's aunt went to see the sub-chaplain, whose name was Julian Young. "I say, Mr Young," she remarked, "this fashion of fainting will degenerate into an epidemic if it is not put a stop to. With your permission I will affix, before next Sunday, this notice in the Cloister . . .

NOTICE

"Whereas a tendency to faint is becoming a prevalent infirmity among young ladies frequenting this chapel, notice is hereby given, that for the future, ladies so affected will no longer be carried out by Sir Horace Seymour, but by Branscombe the dustman."

The habit of fainting in church ceased at once.

CHAPTER TWELVE

Queen Victoria's Reign

"I've often thought I should like to live at Hampton Court. It looks so peaceful and so quiet, and it is such a dear old place to ramble round in the early morning before many people are about. But there, I don't suppose I should really care for it when it came to actual practice. It would be so ghastly dull and depressing in the evening, when your lamp cast uncanny shadows on the panelled walls, and the echo of distant feet rang through the cold stone corridors, and now drew nearer, and now died away, and all was death-like silence, save the beating of one's own heart."

Jerome K. Jerome (1859–1927)

Three Men in a Boat, 1889

Princess Victoria gained her majority (eighteen years) on 24th May 1837, when her uncle William IV was still alive. This fact gave them both a good deal of pleasure – William because Victoria's ambitious mother the Duchess of Kent was thereby prevented from ever becoming regent, and Victoria because she was a determined young woman who was looking forward to her freedom. Up to the time of her accession (20th June 1837) she was dominated by her mother, who would not let her consort much with her "wicked" uncle nor even with his gentle wife Adelaide, and insisted on Victoria sleeping in her room. One of Victoria's first acts as queen was to have her bed moved into a room of her own. Then she wrote a letter of condolence to her Aunt Adelaide (of whom she had always been fond), and shortly afterwards offered her accommodation at Bushey House, Hampton Court. This became Queen Adelaide's residence for the rest of her life (she died in 1849), and here in 1844 she entertained Victoria with her husband and various other crowned heads of Europe at an al fresco lunch in the pheasantry.

"I find Queen Victoria perfect in manner, dignity and grace, with great youthfulness and joyousness", wrote a lady invited to Court (Harriet, Countess Greville, 28th February 1839). For the first couple of years of her reign, young Victoria thoroughly enjoyed being queen; now she could stay up dancing far into the night, upbraid her attendants whenever the whim took her, and (until disenchantment set in) generally had the feeling that she could do very much as she pleased.

It was probably in this mood of defiant ebullience that she decided to open Hampton Court to the public. The Palace had even before this attracted a good deal of interest. It was the subject of enthusiastic articles in *The Mirror of Literature, Amusement and Instruction* (15th August 1829), *The Tourist* (31st December 1833) and *The Penny Magazine of the Society for the Diffusion of Useful Knowledge* (25th January 1834). But now, instead of paying a shilling to be taken round by an impatient under-housekeeper rattling her keys, the public were to be admitted free of charge.

The transition to public opening was made smoother by the death in April 1838 of Lady Emily Montague, the housekeeper. She was the last housekeeper to rely on visitors' fees for her income. There was still the office of housekeeper* but it was salaried, and guides were appointed to show people round. The Palace was closed for a few months so that the state apartments could be made ready, and then opened to the public the following November.

It was during this period when the Palace was closed that a murder took place within its walls. The 12th Company of Lancers was stationed in the barracks near the front gates. On 21st June a private by the name of John Rickey had been to the races and returned much the worse for drink. A Sergeant Hamilton and another sergeant attempted to arrest him, but he grabbed a pair of loaded pistols. The two officers gave chase, but Rickey turned and fired, hitting Sergeant Hamilton who died within a few days. The sentence of death passed on Rickey was afterwards commuted to one of life imprisonment.

Meanwhile it was realized that the Palace had become rather dilapidated and various repairs were set in hand. The sash windows which had inappropriately been set into parts of the old Tudor building were taken out and replaced with casements.

185

* For the housekeeper Mrs Grundy, and Mrs Grundy's Gallery, see Appendix, page 214.

Chimneys were rebuilt, there was much re-cutting and replacing of stonework, the gardens were tidied up and the trees pruned. The Chapel roof was restored, and a major scheme was carried out in the Great Hall. The hammerbeam roof was repainted, the walls re-hung with tapestry, and also (less commendably) the Galyon Hone stained glass was taken out and replaced with glass by Thomas Willement. It is likely that the original windows were in a bad state of repair, and when they were removed some of the glass was given to (or was appropriated by) Lord Hastings – who set it up in his north-country home; later it was moved to the village church of Earsdon (Tyne and Wear), where it may still be seen. The Willement glass was installed in 1843 (the east and west windows) and 1847 (the side windows). It is mainly heraldic and includes the coats-of-arms of all six of Henry VIII's wives. The effect is cheerful and lively, even if one cannot help regretting the removal of the original glass.

The opening of the Palace free to the general public was greeted with wild enthusiasm and celebrated in the press. "A visit to Hampton Court Palace", wrote William Howitt, "is one of the bravest pleasures that a party of happy friends can promise themselves. Especially it is calculated to charm the thousands of pleasure-seekers from the dense and dusty vastness of London . . . Its ample and delightful gardens, bounded by the splendid masses of its lime-tree avenues; its ancient courts, with all their historical recollections; its accumulated paintings, the Cartoons themselves being part of them – are all thrown open to the leisure and perfect enjoyment of the public. There is no royal palace in England, excepting Windsor, which . . . is to be compared with it; and this is, as it should be, given up to the use and enjoyment of the people."

Sir Henry Cole, writing under the name of "Felix Summerly" was even more effusive:

"How many and how various are these ennobling and exhilerating delights! Nature's works and man's bravest achievements go hand in hand together here. Space bounded by art, which crowds can never rob of solitude! Trees never leafless; verdure and brightness omnipresent! . . . Beauty of scene is near at hand, and

stretching as far distant as sight can reach. The trilling music of waters; the magnificent in architecture; the matchless in painting; and best of all, the throng of happy faces (the statist tells you they exceed 30,000 a month in summer), abandoned to mirth, and oblivious of dull care and toil left behind them!''

Although the Palace was open all the year round (as it still is) the most popular season was the summer, particularly the months of July and August – in August 1842, for instance, 50,000 visitors came. The most popular day of the week was (as it still is) Sunday. There was a good deal of protest about this. The Sabbatarian movement was strong in the early years of Victoria's reign and there was loud outcry against what they proclaimed to be the profanation of the British Sunday. But for the previous century the current resident housekeeper had always found it profitable to open the Palace on Sundays after morning service

Summer Noon at Hampton Court
This early Victorian print gives an idyllic view of visitors besporting themselves in the garden after the Palace had been opened to the public. Part of the East Front may be seen and the Tudor Tennis Court. The trees have been left romantically unkempt.

187

— shilling after shilling came her way from appreciative visitors. Therefore a precedent had been established. For the rest of the nineteenth century the Palace was closed on Fridays in order to give the staff a day of rest, and opened every Sunday at 2 p.m.

Getting to the Palace, however, was quite a problem and required ingenuity, patience and expense. One could, of course, do the whole journey by carriage, or by boat. The branch-line of the railway was not built until 1849, and Kingston two miles to the east was the nearest station. Coming from the metropolis, some visitors would take the "fourpenny steamer" from London Bridge to Richmond, then catch the train, South Western line, to Kingston (for Hampton Court), pay their toll to cross Kingston Bridge, and walk from there "through delightful lanes" to the Palace. Alternatively they could take the omnibus (horse-drawn) and travel via Kensington, over Hammersmith Bridge, through Barnes, Richmond, Petersham and Ham as far as Kingston Bridge. There, neatly dodging the toll, they could hire a punt and do the rest of the journey by river.

By Edwardian days new routes had opened up.* The Underground had reached Hammersmith, so one could take the tube as far as that, get out and change to a tram (the tram-stop was opposite the Hop Poles public house). Trams ran every twenty minutes at a speed of eight to ten miles per hour, and took one via Kew Bridge and Twickenham to Bushey Park; the ride would take a little over an hour and cost sixpence single or a shilling return. Then one walked across the Park, admiring the deer and the chestnut trees, and approached the Palace from the north. Otherwise one could go by train from Waterloo to Wimbledon, and take the tram from there, travelling via Kingston, and the tram-ride cost threepence single or sixpence return. The more energetic visitors, however, were by that time arriving by bicycle. Cycles could be left for a small fee in the care of an attendant at the Lion Gate; thereafter visiting the Palace was still free, apart from a nominal charge for the Maze.

Some of the Grace and Favour residents were resentful of the public being admitted so freely to the Palace, since it interfered with their peace and quiet. Admittedly, there was some damage

* *Weekly Ramble*, "Trips on the Tram", 17th August 1907

caused to the gardens during the first few years. But by the end of the century visitors to Hampton Court seem to have behaved much more decorously and taken some account of the notices put up:

"The Public is expected to protect what is intended for the public enjoyment."

Among the many visitors who came shortly after the Palace was opened was the playwright and practical joker Theodore Hook.* He had come to see one of the residents who was a friend of his. The two of them had walked to the far end of Chestnut Avenue in Bushey Park, and were standing by the Teddington lodge-gate. It was a particularly warm July day, and they were both hot and tired and wishing there were an easy way back to the Palace. Then Hook noticed a group of ordinary day-trippers from London; they had been picknicking in the Park and were on their way back to the Palace. As soon as they drew close, Hook suddenly staggered and fell to the ground. Thinking he was ill, the Londoners ran to help him, and started to discuss among themselves what they could use to transport him across the Park. Finally they decided to borrow a door from the lodge. The prostrate Theodore Hook was deposited on it, and four young men of the party carried him all the way down Chestnut Avenue, across the road and up to the Lion Gates. Then to their astonishment, Hook swung his legs to the ground, stood up, raised his hat, thanked the exhausted young men and wished them a very good morning. They were naturally furious, but cooled off a little when they were told who had tricked them – Hook being quite a celebrity.

Nearly all the property in the vicinity of the Palace belonged to the Crown, including the houses over-looking the Green. In 1858 one of these was offered to the famous scientist and professor of chemistry Michael Faraday. Prince Albert had persuaded the Queen that he would be a worthy recipient. Faraday hesitated at first as he was not sure if he had the means to maintain the property. Assured, however, that all necessary work would be done free of charge, he accepted and lived there until his death in 1867. The building was named Faraday House.

189

---

* Theodore Hook, 1788–1841, wrote numerous comic operas and melodramas before accepting the position of Treasurer of the Island of Mauritius. Misappropriating public funds, he lived there in splendour until he was arrested and brought back to England. He was cleared of the charge, but imprisoned for debt. No doubt his finances were still in a precarious state at the time of the incident at Hampton Court.

Another famous resident at Hampton Court was Princess Frederica of Hanover. In 1880 she and her husband were given a suite of rooms on the West Front. There was great rejoicing when in the following year her daughter was born. The baby was called Victoria after the Queen – who came herself to visit them at the Palace. Unfortunately the child died when she was only three weeks old. The Princess devoted herself to good works, and decided to found a convalescent home for women who had recently given birth. An entertainment was given in the Great Hall of the Palace in order to raise funds, and "Princess Frederica's Convalescent Home" was established just outside the walls at the Kingston end of the Park.

In 1865 the Raphael Cartoons and the Tijou Screens were removed to South Kensington were material was being gathered to furnish the museum that would later be known as the Victoria and Albert, or the V & A. It was maintained that they would be better preserved in this new setting.*

At the Palace meanwhile the archway under Wolsey's Gatehouse was given a carved stone ceiling, designed by Lessels in the same style as that over the Anne Boleyn Gateway. A pair of massive oak doors with linenfold panels, dating from the reign of Henry VIII, were discovered serving as a floor to a carpenter's shop, and these were set up under the archway in 1882. This was a great improvement on the cast-iron gates which had stood there previously, but less commendable was the refacing of the Gatehouse in scarlet factory-made brick carried out in the same year. The walls alongside the steps leading to the Great Hall were faced in brick as well, a new set of King's Beasts carved for the pinnacles of the roof, and the stonework decorations on the exterior of the Wren palace were repaired. This was done by a Mr Ruddick, who also restored the Henry VIII coats-of-arms over the archways into the first two courts. The total annual cost of maintaining the whole Palace, including salaries and services, was judged in 1882 to be £8,700.

In the 1880s two serious fires broke out. The first was in 1882. At half-past seven in the morning of 14th December a servant called Mrs Lucas was secretly making tea over a spirit-lamp in

* The Cartoons remained; a new room was provided for them when the present museum building was opened by Edward VII in 1909; but the Tijou screens were later restored to the Palace.

her bedroom. This was situated in the round-window storey (above the small room that lies between the Queen's Gallery and George II's Private Chamber). Mrs Lucas rushed out and raised the alarm. The Palace Fire-Brigade,* assisted by the men of the 4th Hussars and their captain, Ramsay, (then quartered in the barracks) rapidly brought the fire under control. But unfortunately Mrs Lucas had gone back into the room to fetch something, and she was found suffocated by the fumes.

Apart from the loss of life, not much damage had been done. The fabric was repaired at a cost of £4,000. The Palace was inspected from a safety point of view. Hot-water-pipe central heating was put in to replace the coke fires which had previously warmed the state rooms, and an electric fire-alarm system was installed. In addition lowering gear was provided to facilitate the speedy removal of valuable pictures and tapestries in case of fire.

It was just as well that all these precautions had been taken, for another fire of much greater extent occurred in 1886. This was in the rooms north of Chapel Court which had been Edward VI's nursery, but had been largely rebuilt in the eighteenth century. The fire started in the morning of 19th November – a servant had left a candle burning in a dark closet, the candle set the wooden panelling alight, and it was three and a half hours before the blaze could be put out. One of the residents in that part of the Palace was an invalid, and she had to be rescued from her rooms by being carried over the roof by one of the warders.† In all nearly forty rooms were burnt, though many of them were small, having been subdivided by wooden partitions – in fact these inflammable partitions seem to have been the chief cause of the spread of the fire. The more solid shell of the original building survived, and afterwards the damaged apartments were restored, or rebuilt, in the Tudor style, at a cost of £8,000. All the residents were now asked to contribute towards the insurance of the building, and also to pay a special water-rate. The latter helped to fund an extra high-pressure water supply to the Palace, with hydrants throughout the building, ready to deal speedily with any future fires.

191

* At this time, the Brigade consisted of a Superintendent and eighteen men, six of whom were resident in the Palace.
† The lady's name was Miss Somerset, and her rescuer's Mr Thorne. He was afterwards given the medal of the Humane Society.

CHAPTER THIRTEEN

Twentieth Century

"'Hampton Court,' said Bernard. 'Hampton Court. This is our meeting-place. Behold the red chimneys, the square battlements of Hampton Court. The tone of my voice as I say "Hampton Court" proves that I am middle-aged. Ten years, fifteen years ago, I should have said "Hampton Court?" with interrogation – what will it be like? Will there be lakes, mazes? Or with anticipation, what is going to happen to me here? Whom shall I meet? Now, Hampton Court – Hampton Court – the words beat a gong in the space I have so laboriously cleared with half a dozen telephone messages and postcards, give off ring after ring of sound, booming, sonorous; and pictures rise – summer afternoons, boats, old ladies holding their skirts up, one urn in winter, some daffodils in March – these all float to the top of the waters that now lie deep on every scene.'"

Virginia Woolf (1882–1941)

The Waves

No great changes came with the turn of the century. The Grace and Favour ladies – they were nearly all ladies by now – continued to inhabit their apartments in gentility and quietness. Mostly they were widows or other close relatives of men who had achieved some eminence in public service. On the whole they were moderately well off, and those who were not would often decline or resign the honour. For although the actual accommodation was rent-free, the heating, lighting and cleaning had to be paid for, as well as the rates and insurance, also there were various subscriptions one could not easily avoid. Many of the residents were old friends even before they came, so there naturally developed a feeling of community. This being the case, the Palace inhabitants had developed their own customs. One of these was the use of a type of sedan-chair on wheels called a "push". In this ladies were carried from one part of the building to another when paying visits in the evening. Another custom,

'One Urn in Winter'
A late 17th-century urn,
probably by Gaius Gabriel
Cibber.

which has only recently died out, was that of letting a basket down on a string from the upper storeys in order to collect groceries, correspondence or small parcels, and then hauling it up again.

For most of the nineteenth century, none of the interior of Wolsey's palace had been seen by the public. The Wolsey Closet had been a butler's pantry before it was opened to view in 1890, and the Wolsey Rooms* were still used as a Grace and Favour apartment until they were restored and opened to the public in 1923.

The first major discovery in the Palace in the twentieth century was the excavation of the old moat bridge by the West Front. The moat originally surrounded the whole building, and this part had been filled in at the end of the seventeenth century. In 1689 a labourer called Arnold Thompson was employed ''shovelling

193

* These rooms were traditionally known as the Lord Cardinal's Lodgings. Though in the first place they were probably used by his guests or his servants, after he gave the Palace to Henry VIII Wolsey seems to have used them himself.

and wheeling 240½ yards of Rubbish out of the Passage by the Kitchens and laying the same in the Mote by the Great Gate." For two hundred years there was flat ground as one approached the West Front of the Palace. Then in 1908 it was decided to excavate to see whether there was any evidence of the old moat beneath the roadway. Various objects were unearthed, including two Elizabethan pewter dishes, a Dutch silver spoon of 1700 and an inferior metal spoon of the same date, a brass toy cannon, also crockery and floor tiles. But the most exciting discovery was Henry VIII's bridge with its five arches of Headington stone, preserved almost intact where it had lain beneath the surface. A crenellated parapet was made, and a set of King's Beasts carved,* creating the striking entrance we know today.

Work was done in the grounds to equip them better for the entertainment of the public. The five hundred deer that used to browse in Home Park had already been moved out (March 1890), and in 1924 the old tiltyards, which had been used for growing vegetables since William III's time, were turned into rose-gardens. At the same time the surviving tiltyard tower was made into a restaurant.

Up to 1968 the gardens were open all night, with just two men on watch in the state apartments. Now security is much tighter altogether, a bag-check in the Great Gatehouse.

In 1922 an inspection was made of the roof of the Great Hall, and it was found to be so riddled with dry rot and death-watch beetle that it was actually on the point of collapse. For instance, one of the principal supporting beams, measuring 1 foot 9 inches by 9 inches in girth, was so eaten away that it was nothing but a hollow shell. Accordingly a major repair on the timber-work was put in hand and completed by 1927 (a report on it was published in *The Builder* of that date).

The bridge that had been built across the Thames in 1865 was a cast iron one – Ernest Law described it as "one of the ugliest bridges in England" – and at first tolls continued to be exacted by the successors of the owner of the first Georgian bridge, James Clarke. However in 1876 the Metropolitan Board of Works purchased it for £50,000, and on 8th July it was made "free for ever".

194

---

* A new set of King's beasts were carved in 1950.

This bridge survived until 1933, when the present brick one was built. It was opened by the Prince of Wales, later to reign briefly as Edward VIII.

The Palace survived the Second World War virtually unscathed, despite the dropping of incendiary bombs and one or two high-explosive and delayed-action bombs in the vicinity. One incendiary was dropped near the Tudor Tennis Court, causing some damage there. The resident curator at this time was E. J. Rainbow.* On the staff of the Lord Chamberlain's department, he was appointed in 1930 and before that had been twenty years at Buckingham Palace. In 1932 he organized a Salvage Corps of twelve men on a part-time basis. If a fire should break out anywhere in the Palace their task was to remove as quickly as possible any pictures, tapestries, furnishings and carpets that seemed endangered, and to do their best to ensure that water damage was kept to a minimum. Thanks to them, and to the efficiency of the fire precautions in general, the Palace was preserved more or less intact. The war over, a National Savings Conference was held in the Great Hall in 1946, attended by nearly four hundred delegates.

Hampton Court Palace continued to house (as it does to this day) some Grace and Favour residents, though rather fewer than in previous centuries. Among the more notable was the Grand-Duchess Xenia of Russia, sister of the ill-fated Czar Nicholas II, who together with his family was shot by the Red Guard in 1918. The Grand-Duchess however lived quietly in Wilderness House by the Maze at Hampton Court until she died, aged eighty-five, in 1936. An even more celebrated Grace and Favour resident was Lady Baden-Powell, the founder of the Girl Guides and Brownies, and she also spent her retirement at the Palace, in the rooms overlooking Base Court and approached by the staircase at the back of the Great Hall.

In 1962 cleaning of the painted panels, depicting the Passion, in the Wolsey Closet revealed that under at least part of the sixteenth-century pigment, is work of fifteenth-century date. This dates from the time of the Knights Hospitallers and is a rare survival of pre-Wolsey Hampton Court.

195

* Mr Rainbow also spent his retirement in the Palace, and died there in 1983

An even more important conservation project was the cleaning and restoration of the Mantegna *Triumph of Caesar* canvases. This was begun in 1962, and took thirteen years to complete.* The paintings, probably in better state now than they have been for over three hundred years, are displayed in controlled atmospheric conditions in the Orangery, together with a fine second-century sarcophagus and Roman reliefs on loan from the British Museum, and classical busts based on Roman originals, belonging to the Royal Collection. Visitors to the Orangery may be surprised to meet a venerable cat who regards the paintings with an almost proprietorial air; her name is Trixie and she is at least twenty-two years old.†

In 1969 a new aluminium-framed glass-house was constructed to house the Great Vine, at a cost of £8,000. According to measurements done in March 1962, the trunk of the vine has a girth of 7 feet 1 inch at ground level and of 6 feet 2 inches a foot above the ground. It is under the expert care of Mrs Peto, who has been looking after it since 1960. In an average year it produces now 450–500 pounds of grapes; in a bumper year, such as 1977, over 700 pounds.

Work continued, and continues, to be done around the Palace; in fact it never stops. The Astronomical Clock was restored in 1947 and the bells cleaned and re-hung. In January 1976, having been left unwound since the previous May, the clock was electrified. In 1976–7 a major restoration was undertaken of the hammerbeam roof in the Great Hall. Fountain Court was cleaned in 1978, and in 1981 the restoration of the chimney-stacks by Dove Brothers of Islington won the award of the R.I.B.A., beating over 230 other entries. A new shop was opened in July 1979, with its entrance under the Anne Boleyn Gateway, and the "Care of Buildings" exhibition established in the south-west corner of the Palace was officially opened by the Duke of Gloucester in May 1983. At the time of writing, the floors in the King's Private Apartments are being replaced, and a lift installed by the Prince of Wales's landing.

As well as caring for the existing building, archaeological excavations have been carried out to try to discover more about

---

* For details of the work, see Appendix, page 215.
† Another interesting cat resident in the Palace belonged to Lady Paget in c. 1893. It was called "Barrister" and lived on an entirely vegetarian diet.

Tudor-style Chimneys
Although largely rebuilt they retain a fantastic assortment of patterns; their restoration won
an R.I.B.A. award in 1981.

the Palace in past centuries. Partly prompted by the investigations of an amateur water-diviner, Lady Paisley, a dig was undertaken in Clock Court to find the exact site of Wolsey's Palace. It was revealed that there had been a whole range of buildings running east-west, parallel with and hidden by Wren's colonnade. It was also established that the Manor House of the Knights Hospitallers ran north-south, facing the river, and not east-west as had been thought previously.

Another dig was carried out ten years later by the Central Excavation Unit. There were two sites; one was in the east range of Clock Court to the south of the George II gateway. Here until 1732 there were said to have been two sets of bay-windows; the excavation brought forth some abraided Tudor brick and window mullions of Reigate stone, which helps to confirm this. The other site excavated was in Lady Mornington's Garden before it was re-turfed: the purpose was to find the position of the Queen's Gallery built for Anne Boleyn and the alignment of the moat. The subsequent report* maintained that the wall originally intended to be the wall of the moat was never used as such, but when the building of the Queen's Gallery began it became the foundation of its west wall, and the moat was finally sited further to the east.

At the beginning of the century admission to the State Rooms was still free. By 1950 visitors had to pay one shilling a head on weekdays, sixpence on Saturdays, half-price for children, but it was still free on Sundays and bank holidays, and lecture-tours were provided at no extra charge. The cost of admission gradually rose, and came to be charged at all times when the State Rooms were open, with reductions for children and pensioners, and further reductions in the winter months.

Admission to the gardens, kitchens, Tudor Tennis Court and the Great Vine remains free, so there is no means of counting the thousands of people (an estimated 60% of all visitors) who come to see these only. In 1982, approximately 467,000 people paid for entrance to the State Apartments, while in 1981 the figure was higher, some 524,000 (perhaps the fact that it was the year of the royal wedding had something to do with it). The figures are rising still.

198

* By D. Batchelor, *Post-Mediaval Archaeology*, Vol, II 1977, pp 36–49

The Palace is normally open all the year round, but in November 1982 it was closed to the public for three days while Queen Beatrix and the royal family of the Netherlands entertained our Queen Elizabeth II and the royal family of this country to a banquet. The Dutch party brought their own silver, china and glass for this occasion, and they provided many yards of rich carpet to cover the floors of the Great Hall and the Great Watching Chamber. The Queen's Guardroom and Presence Chamber were renovated and after the visit opened to the public.

From time to time Hampton Court is visited by royalty, sometimes formally, sometimes informally; though it is not, like Windsor Castle, used for prolonged stays nor, like Buckingham Palace, very much a royal residence and therefore not open to the public. Hampton Court Palace, however complex, however remote from the lives of most of us, remains accessible, a treasure-house of many things, not least of which is history.

The Royal Collection at the Palace

"I can make any number of men of title
but I cannot make a Holbein."
      attributed to Henry VIII

A tapestry will stop a draught, a portrait will convey a likeness as no description can. But the collecting and commissioning of works of art were also done for reasons of self-aggrandizement or (to put it at a slightly higher level) the desire to have fine things around one. Such were the motives that prompted Wolsey in forming his fabulous collection of tapestries. Henry VIII too felt he owed it to the dignity of his position to extend a measure of encouragement to the arts and at the same time indulge his love of display. He was never a great patron, in the style of Lorenzo de'Medici or Francis I, and his interest in painting was confined almost exclusively to portraiture, yet he does seem to have perceived, albeit dimly, that in Hans Holbein he was employing an artist of exceptional talent.

Holbein first came to England at the suggestion of the great scholar and humanist Erasmus, who sent him to his friend the equally great Sir Thomas More with a letter of introduction: "he is coming to England to scrape a few angels together." More replied, "I am afraid he won't find England as fruitful as he had hoped", and it was not until Holbein's second and final stay that he was able to secure the patronage of the Court.

There were certain practical reasons why Henry VIII commissioned portraits – and these held good at least for the rest of the Tudor dynasty. First, there was a need for a definitive image of the monarch. This should be both recognizable and memorable, presenting not only a true likeness but preferably an aura of majesty as well. This definitive image might be copied, with or without variations, and such portraits were often exchanged with other monarchs. They might be of the king himself or of his family; Mabuse's *Children of Christian II* is an example. Portraits were also made in connexion with putative marriages; Holbein was sent more than once to portray possible brides for Henry VIII, and the full-length figure of Edward VI by Guillim Stretes or Scrotes* probably dates from about 1550 when there were negotiations for the thirteen-year-old boy to marry the eldest daughter of the King of France.

There is a family portrait at Hampton Court, probably painted for Henry VIII after the fall and execution of Catherine Howard; it shows the King with his three children, two of his servants and, interestingly, a posthumous portrait of Jane Seymour. The King had paintings done to celebrate his victories as well as his dynasty. Associated with the above picture are works depicting the Battle of the Spurs, the Field of Cloth of Gold, and the King's embarkation to France in 1544. Of earlier date is another view of the Battle of the Spurs, focusing on the meeting of Henry VIII with his ally Maximilian I, head of the Holy Roman Empire.†

Henry had inventories made of the Royal Collection in 1542 and 1547; the latter included the bitterly satirical work by Girolamo da Treviso of the four evangelists stoning the Pope (this was painted in London at the commission of the King).

When Nicholas Hillyarde was first employed to paint Elizabeth I's picture in miniature, she advised him to portray her in an open garden so that her features would be delineated in line rather than shadow. No doubt she considering it more flattering, and most of the other portraits of the Queen, including the anonymous one at Hampton Court (dating probably from the 1580s), continued to be executed with this principle in mind. Again, she may not have been a great patron of the visual arts, yet when the Duke of Wirtemberg visited the Palace in 1592 he was impressed. "Many of the splendid large rooms", he wrote, "are embellished with masterly paintings", and he noticed how these were protected with curtains made of squares of yellow and white silk.

It was not until the reign of James I that, almost for the first

201

---

* Holbein died of plague in 1543, and Streets succeeded him as court-painter, at a salary of £62 per annum.
† For none of thes works is the artist's name recorded.

time in this country, art began to be valued and collected for its own sake. The King himself took only a passing interest. His court-painter after about 1618 was Daniel Mytens,* who was employed almost exclusively as a portraitist. Queen Anne of Denmark, on the other hand, not only offered considerable patronage to living artists, such as Inigo Jones, who designed for her architecture and the settings of court masques in which she loved to perform herself, but began to collect paintings for their own intrinsic merits. Lord Salisbury went so far as to say that she preferred pictures to the company of living people (probably an overstatement, for she was a gregarious person). Her full-length portrait at the Palace is by Paul van Somer from Antwerp, but the paintings she seems to have preferred to collect were mainly still-lifes and small cabinet-paintings such as *Christ in the House of Martha and Mary* by Vredeman de Vries.†

The Queen's enthusiasm was shared by her elder son Henry. A latter-day Renaissance prince, he took an interest in aesthetic matters as well as in sports and feats of arms. It is not entirely easy to discover which works were in the Prince's collection, though he is said to have bought important Venetian, as well as Flemish and Dutch paintings. Two anonymous paintings at Hampton Court are known to have belonged to him, the *Battle of Pavia* and the (probably Flemish) *Boy Looking through a Casement*.

When Prince Henry died his collection was given to his younger brother Charles, who also inherited their mother's paintings. Charles I was to become the greatest patron of the arts of all British monarchs. In developing his taste he was helped and inspired principally by two courtiers, the Earl of Arundel and George Villiers Duke of Buckingham. It was through Arundel that the Leonardo drawings came to Windsor Castle, and he helped to bring Van Dyck over to this country in 1620. Buckingham had a fine gallery of art at York House, surpassing even the Royal Collection at this time. It will have encouraged in young Charles a love of Venetian paintings in which it was especially rich. "He loves old paintings, especially those of our province and city", observed the Venetian ambassador. Buckingham also

* Daniel Mytens (*c.* 1590–before 1648) came from The Hague, where he was probably a pupil of Miereveld.
† Hans Vredeman de Vries, a Fleming, is best remembered for his furniture pattern-book of *c.* 1580 and his introduction of strapwork design.

afforded patronage to living artists; Honthorst and Rubens.

In 1623, when he was still Prince of Wales, Charles went with Buckingham to the Court of Philip IV of Spain – his father was trying to negotiate a Spanish marriage for him. The marriage plans came to nothing but artistically the visit was a most formative experience. Charles had the opportunity of seeing Philip IV's wonderful collection, and the King presented him with Titian's *Venus of the Pardo*. It was on this visit too that Charles arranged to buy the Raphael Cartoons.

Raphael drew the Cartoons as designs for tapestries intended for the Sistine Chapel in the Vatican, and their theme is the Acts of the Apostles. When the purchase was completed in 1632 they were brought to Hampton Court (where William III was later to have the Cartoon Gallery built to house them), and there they remained until 1865.

On his accession Charles appointed Daniel Mytens as "picture-drawer of our Chamber in ordinarie". Mytens had been born in Delft, and was introduced to Court circles by the Earl of Arundel. Paintings by his hand at Hampton Court include the group-portrait of Charles I, Henrietta Maria and the King's dwarf Sir Jeffrey Hudson (dating from 1630–32), the double portrait of the royal couple with a laurel wreath (of similar date), and a self-portrait. Mytens also painted a portrait of the dwarf on his own; Charles I commissioned this picture of Sir Jeffrey dressed in a red suit against a wooded background and paid the artist £40 for it.

Successful portraitist though he was, Mytens was clearly not in the same league as Rubens or Van Dyck. Rubens visited this country on a diplomatic mission in 1629. By then Charles owned paintings by, for example, Titian, Tintoretto, Schiavone, Bassano and Veronese. Rubens was much impressed with Charles, whom he called "the greatest amateur of painting among the princes of the world", and also with his collection, commenting on "the incredible quantity of excellent pictures, statues and ancient inscriptions which are to be found in this Court". Rubens was then commissioned to paint the nine canvases for the ceiling of Inigo Jones's recently erected Banqueting House at Whitehall.

Self Portrait by Raphael
For years designated 'School of Urbino', this painting has been revealed by recent research to be an original portrait of the artist as a young man.

Temporarily, until the Rubens paintings arrived, it is possible that the large composition of *Apollo and Diana* by Gerrit van Honthorst (now over the Queen's Staircase at Hampton Court) was propped up to decorate this same Banqueting House. The theme suggests that of a masque. Mercury (represented by the Duke of Buckingham) is introducing the liberal arts to Apollo and Diana (the King and Queen); there is a preliminary drawing for this work in the Boymans Museum at Rotterdam, but in this the element of portraiture has been left out. Honthorst came to London in 1628 and the work was commissioned, by the King, at that time; he had possibly been introduced to the Court through Elizabeth of Bohemia, Charles I's sister.

However, the artist with whose name Charles I is most closely associated is undoubtedly Van Dyck. Anthony Van Dyck had been Rubens's assistant in Antwerp. He settled in London in 1632, when the King knighted him, and gave him a house in Blackfriars and a pension of £200 a year. No royal portraits by this artist hang at Hampton Court, but there is a painting of Van Dyck's quick-tempered mistress Margaret Lemon (once in a fit of jealous fury she tried to bite off his thumb), and also a posthumous portrait of Lady Venetia Digby.* Van Dyck worked for the Court until his death in 1641.

Queen Henrietta Maria encouraged the coming to England of the Italian artist Orazio Gentileschi – together with his painter daughter Artemesia – and commissioned him to paint panels to decorate the hall ceiling of the newly completed Queen's House at Greenwich (these were later removed by Duchess Sarah to Marlborough House). At Hampton Court is his *Joseph and Potiphar's Wife*. The Queen was a Roman Catholic and liked to have religious paintings around her; one of her collection was Holbein's *Noli Me Tangere*.

The King's collection, which came to include works of such primary importance as Titian's *Girl in a Fur Cloak*, Raphael's *La Perla*, Mantegna's *Dead Christ* and Caravaggio's *Death of the Virgin*, was looked after by Abraham van der Doort, who received a salary of £40 a year for life, until he committed suicide in 1640.

The greatest acquisition of all Charles I's fabulous collection

---

* Lady Venetia was a famous courtesan, described by John Aubrey (*Brief Lives*) as a ''most beautiful desireable Creature''. She was mistress to the Earl of Dorset, then in 1625 married Sir Kenelm Digby (whose portrait is also at Hampton Court).

was the series of paintings by Mantegna, The *Triumph of Caesar* – by far the most important series of Italian Renaissance paintings to be seen outside Italy. This is still at Hampton Court Palace. Charles's agents Nicholas Lanier (Master of the King's Music and jack of several trades) and Daniel Nys (a Dutch merchant and art-dealer) had already been engaged in buying a number of paintings, including those listed above, from the collection of the dukes of Mantua – whose line was dying out and who were virtually bankrupt. The cost of these works was £15,000. Then negotiations were begun to buy the *Triumph of Caesar* for a further £10,500.

Mantegna was working on this series of paintings, done in tempera on canvas, in about 1486–1494, for the Marchese Francesco Gonzaga. Mantegna had been enticed to the court of Mantua by Frencesco's grandfather, Lodovico, and for him had painted the Camera degli Sposi in the Ducal Palace, including portraits of the Gonzaga family. The commissioning of a work depicting a triumphal procession in classical Rome stemmed from the Gonzaga's antiquarian interests and was a congenial one for Mantegna who shared them. Originally the nine paintings may have been intended to be seen through the interstices of a colonnade, and the composition is linked from one canvas to the next. They were probably hung about five feet above the ground.

The purchase of the paintings was completed in 1627, and they left the city (fortunately) before it was sacked by the Imperial forces in 1630. When they arrived in England they were brought straight to Hampton Court and hung in the King's Gallery of the old Tudor Palace. At various times they have been moved from one part of the building to another, and it is possible that they may once have been taken to Mortlake for tapestries to be made from them; apart from that, they have never left Hampton Court.

Had Charles I's collection remained intact there would be nothing to rival it anywhere in the world. But with the turmoil of the Civil War and the stern times of the Protectorate, it suffered great depredations. When the King was under house arrest at Hampton Court in 1647, he entrusted his collection of miniatures to the Keeper of the Privy Lodgings for safe keeping – apparently

'The Vase Bearer'
From the 'Triumph of Caesar' canvases by Andrea Mantegna

207

he was confident that he would see them again. After the King's execution in 1649 an inventory was made listing and valuing all his effects. At the same time a group of trustees was set up to search for works which might have been embezzled or had otherwise disappeared. The total value of the collection from all his palaces was put at £37,000. Raphael's *La Perla* (sold to Spain and now in the Prado) was thought worth £2,000, the Raphael Cartoons £300, Caravaggio's *Death of the Virgin* (now in the Louvre) £150, the Holbein portraits of Erasmus and Johannes Frobenius £200 the pair, Van Dyck's *Cupid and Psyche* £110, the *Embarkation of Henry VIII* £26, Mabuse's *Adam and Eve* £50, the *Family of Henry VIII* (sold to Colonel Webb but later restored to Hampton Court) £15, Hans Eworth's *Elizabeth and the Three Goddesses* £3, and a Rembrandt self-portrait no more than £5.

Many of the paintings were sold, some to individuals in this country, some abroad, and the first £30,000 of the money was passed to the Treasurer of the Navy to build up the fleet. Works which were retained by Cromwell, and are still to be seen at Hampton Court, included — as well as the Raphael Cartoons and the *Triumph of Caesar* — Bronzino's *Lady in Green*, Titian's *The Lovers*, Tintoretto's *Esther and Ahasuerus* and *The Nine Muses*, Correggio's *Holy Family*, the head of a shepherd boy attributed to Giorgione, and works by Joos van Cleve, Bassano and Dosso Dossi.

After the Restoration, steps were taken to retrieve the paintings wherever possible (this was supervised by John Webb and Emmanuel de Critz), and an Act of Pardon, Indemnity and Oblivion was passed on 29th August 1660, exonerating all possessors of royal property as long as it was returned by the end of September. Then another inventory was drawn up towards the end of the decade; about 210 paintings are listed as being at Hampton Court — the *Triumph of Caesar* canvases were in the King's Gallery, full-length portraits in the Queen's Gallery,* and small works in the King's Closet. When in 1663 Charles II was asked about his collection by Balthasar de Monconnys, he said he was delighted to show the enquirer what he had, but regretted that "it was not one half of what his father had owned".

* This was still the Tudor Palace; neither gallery now exists.

Peter Lely was appointed Principal Painter to Charles II in 1661, but it was Anne Hyde, Duchess of York, who commissioned the portraits of langorous almond-eyed ladies known as the *Windsor Beauties*,* which now hang in the Communication Gallery. The original set was of eleven paintings. Among them is Barbara Villiers Duchess of Castlemaine, the King's principal mistress and an ancestress of Diana, Princess of Wales. The others are Frances Stuart, Elizabeth Hamilton, Jane Needham, Frances and Margaret Brooke, Anne Digby, Henrietta Boyle, Elizabeth Wriothesley and Mary Bagot. (Lely's eleventh portrait, of Louise de Kérouaille, is at Coombe Abbey.) They all have a plump and slightly *déshabillé* charm, what Robert Herrick called ''a sweet disorder of the dress'', and look as if they might be related. ''Good, but not like'' was Samuel Pepys's comment.

Some of the paintings which were intended for Charles I's collection, but had not yet been sent over to this country at the outbreak of the Civil War, were very prudently kept in The Netherlands, by one William Frizell, until the Restoration. From this source Charles II was able to add to the Royal Collection George de la Tour's *St Jerome*, Van Heemskerck's *Jonah under the Gourd*, the *Gentleman in Red* then thought to be a Holbein, and – a most important acquisition – Bruegel's *Massacre of the Innocents*. This last painting also bears the title *Sacking a Village in Winter*. Parts of the composition were at some time overpainted, transforming the dead babies of the first subject into the slaughtered animals of the second, and suggesting a reference to the Spanish occupation of The Netherlands. Apparently the overpainting was done straight on top of Bruegel's original pigment, no layer of varnish between, which makes it hazardous to remove.

At the Restoration also, Charles II was given various paintings by the Dutch States-General. These included two portraits by Lorenzo Lotto (one of them the *Andrea Odoni*), Veronese's *Mystic Marriage of St Catherine*, Parmigianino's *Minerva* and two important paintings by Schiavone, *Judgement of Midas* and *Christ before Pilate*.

It was perhaps in recognition of the kindness he had received

209

---

* So called because of the early 19th century they hung in the Queen's Bedchamber at Windsor Castle.

'Andrea Odoni'
By Lorenzo Lotto. The sitter
was a collector and connoisseur
as the painting suggests. The
work is dated 1527 and was
given to Charles II by the States
of Holland.

from the government of The Netherlands that in 1676 Charles II appointed a Dutchman to the post of "Purveyor and Keeper" of the Royal Collection. He was Gerrit Uylenburgh, a cousin of Rembrandt's wife Saskia; his record was not entirely good – he had been trying to sell fakes to the Elector of Brandenburg. Under Charles he was paid a salary of £100 a year. Another inventory was made when James II came to the throne, and under William III there were two curatorial posts: one designated Keeper and Surveyor (held by Somnius), and the other Mender and Repairer (Parry Walton). Each was paid £200 a year.

The *Hampton Court Beauties*, eight full-length portraits of ladies-in-waiting, were commissioned by Mary II from Godfrey Kneller. Lady Dorchester is said to have tried to dissuade the

'Massacre of the Innocents'
By Pieter Bruegel. This work
was later partly overpainted
and acquired a second title
'Sacking a Village in Winter'.

Queen on the grounds that "if the King was to ask for the portraits of all the wits in his court, would not the rest think he called them fools?" The paintings were much admired by contemporaries and were hung in the Queen's Water Gallery. Defoe commented how delightful it was that there the portraits might be compared with the ladies themselves. It is said that originally there were twelve paintings. They have a formal elegance, and won Kneller a knighthood.* For the King, Kneller painted the large equestrian portrait in the First Presence Chamber.

William's interest in paintings extended to having Parry Walton repair the Raphael Cartoons before they were hung in the Cartoon Gallery made to house them, and to having Louis Laguerre restore the *Triumph of Caesar* canvases. Unfortunately

211

* Now, since the visit of the royal family of The Netherlands, they are displayed to great advantage in the Queen's Guard Room.

Laguerre's idea of restoration was to repaint them heavily in oil-paint on top of the tempera. At the time this met with approval. George Vertue, writing some twenty-five years later, said that he had so "happily mimicked the Master as to complet them to the Great Satisfaction of the King and all the Curious."

All in all, William's interest in art was not altogether advantageous to the Royal Collection for, considering himself more Dutch than English, he removed certain paintings to Holland; two heads by Piero di Cosimo, Van Dyck's self-portrait, *The Young Mother* by Gerard Dou, and two important works by Holbein, *Robert Cheseman* and *Man with a Hawk*.

After William's death Queen Anne, who was mildly interested in the arts (it was she who bought the Bogdani animal and bird pictures now at the Palace), tried without success to get these paintings back. Through her Deputy Chamberlain, Sir John Stanley, she acquired the full-length portrait of a lady in loose oriental costume and pearl-embroidered slippers, erroneously thought for centuries to be a picture of Elizabeth I.

Neither George I nor George II added much to the collection. George II's wife Caroline, however, acquired miniatures by Cowper and Hoskins, and the very fine Holbein portrait of Sir Henry Guildford. She rediscovered the Holbein drawings (now at Windsor), and kept at Kensington a Cabinet Room where the smaller works in her collection were displayed. With her considerable interest in the arts, it is surprising that she did not get on better with her elder son Frederick Prince of Wales, who shared her tastes. The connoisseur George Vertue, who encouraged them both and who compiled an inventory for the Prince, said on the latter's death that he had been the greatest patron of the arts since Charles I.

Prince Frederick bought, as well as works by Claude and Poussin, the Rubens *Summer Landscape*, and miniatures by Isaac Oliver, the two delightful little paintings by Jan or "Velvet" Bruegel, the Teniers landscapes, and (interestingly) Robert Peake's portrait of Prince Henry of Wales hunting with the Earl of Essex – which are still at Hampton Court.

George III bought the large works by Sebastiano Ricci (includ-

Diana de Vere, Duchess of St
Albans
One of the series of 'Hampton
Court Beauties' painted by Sir
Godfrey Kneller for Mary II.

213

ing the *Adoration of the Magi* and *Christ in the House of Simon*), which are looking far more impressive since their recent cleaning. He and his wife Charlotte patronized the portraitist Johann Zoffany, also Gainsborough to some extent, and Benjamin West, and bought Canalettos through Consul Joseph Smith; but because of the King's dislike of the Palace it is not surprising that few of these acquisitions were ever hung at Hampton Court. George IV was a great collector, but for similar reasons, kept the best works for the residences he inhabited himself.

When the Palace was opened to the public by Queen Victoria, the "gratuitous exhibitions"* of such works as the Raphael Cartoons was acclaimed with enthusiasm, for they were thought improving to the mind. But a formidable Lady Housekeeper of the 1840s–50s, called appropriately Mrs Grundy,† considered it was not quite proper for ordinary people to see works of art that portrayed the naked human body. Consequently she imposed her own personal censorship, went round the Palace collecting up any works which she thought unfit for the public to see and shut them away in a particularly dark apartment which became known as Mrs Grundy's Gallery. It is impossible to list all the paintings and sculptures she hid away, but they are known to have included Van Dyck's *Cupid and Psyche*, Cariani's *Venus*, and the leaden statue of Venus now to be seen at the end of the Pond Garden. Mrs Grundy guarded the key like a dragon and would only unlock the door if presented with a written authority from the Lord Chamberlain.

Others had different objections to the display of works of art at Hampton Court. Sir Henry Cole who, with the Prince Consort, was involved in the setting up of the Great Exhibition of 1851, was the founder of the Victoria and Albert Museum and became its first Director in 1860. In 1859 he printed a little booklet, in a limited edition of 150 copies, entitled *Some Thoughts on Hampton Court Palace, its Pictures, Tapestry and Other Works of Decorative Art*. In this he put the view that it had become "little else than a *storehouse* for works of art . . . and the character of the decorations of the Palace has much deteriorated." Paintings had apparently been hung on top of the tapestries and in some cases

---

* These words are from the *Penny Magazine* for September 1841.
† Not the original Mrs Grundy; she was a character referred to but never appearing in Thomas Morton's play *Speed the Plough*, first performed at Covent Garden in 1800 – but remarkably like her all the same.

had actually been nailed through them. "In very few instances", Cole observed, "are the pictures seen well." He was also concerned about the condition of the paintings, woodcarving and metalwork, and above all of the tapestries which he said needed immediate attention. Cole proposed that the Palace should be restored as far as possible to its original state of decoration, and the tapestries should be revealed (it seems that many were covered with calico screens). Cole's view was that all pictures coming into the category of fine art were out of place at Hampton Court and should be brought to the metropolis. (Some of them he wanted for the V & A, no doubt.) There, he said, they would be better seen and better looked after, for "Hitherto when the Crown Pictures have required attention, they have been placed in the hands of picture cleaners, virtually without control . . . a process attended with great mischief."

It was no doubt to Cole's great satisfaction that the Raphael Cartoons were sent to the Victoria and Albert Museum in 1865.[*] As for the condition of the rest of the paintings, it continued to give cause for concern. An article in *The World*, 6th August 1890, described the state of them as "perfectly disgraceful . . . either thick with dust and 'bloomed' varnish, or else scrubbed down and repaired by injudicious 'restorers'."

In the twentieth century efforts were made to do something about the Mantegna *Triumph of Caesar* which had been so heavily overpainted by Laguerre. In about 1913 the writer and critic Roger Fry made an examination of one of the canvases (the *Picture Bearers*); then he attempted to clean off the Laguerre paint and in doing so removed some of Mantegna's as well. At this point he changed tactics and decided to overpaint the picture himself, changing the muscular black Nubian into a white man.

Nothing more was done until 1930, when Kennedy North relined the canvases and attempted to fix down the paint (which was flaking badly, because of the thick layer of oil-paint over the original tempera) by embedding it in an even thicker layer of paraffin wax. Visually the effect of this was to darken the tones and to render the canvases more obscure as the wax lost its transparency. This might have been pardonable, had not the

215

---

* Their place in the Cartoon Gallery was eventually filled when in 1905 Baron Emile d'Erlanger gave to the Royal Collection a set of 17th-century Brussels tapestries done from Raphael's designs.

'Lady in Green'
By Agnolo Bronzino. One of the paintings from the collection of Charles I, it has been cleaned
in recent years.

physical effect on the paintings been so disastrous. In the words of John Brealey, "the very idea of using wax on a tempera painting is outrageous. It had the effect of driving the paint *through* the canvas." In short, the *Triumph* was in such a state that most art-historians thought it a write-off.

The paintings were stored in a shelter behind the Orangery during the Second World War. Then in 1962 they were examined again and a thirteen-year conservation project was embarked upon, under the direction of John Brealey. Incredibly he was able to remove not only the Kennedy North wax (he swore there was over a ton of it), but the Laguerre oil-paint as well. Only the canvas depicting the *Prisoners* was left uncleaned, because there appeared to be hardly any of the Mantegna pigment left. For the rest, Brealey was able to reveal the original tempera paint to an extent little short of miraculous. The restoration was completed in 1975, and the paintings once more displayed in the Orangery, the rear wall of which was taken ten feet back – both temperature and humidity there being now carefully controlled.

As to the smaller paintings in the Palace, after the Second World War King George VI agreed to display his collection of Italian and Northern primitives there. For instance, there was the Lucas Cranach *Apollo and Diana* which had been bought by Prince Albert, and the Gentile da Fabriano *Madonna and Child with Angels*, bought by Queen Victoria as a present for him. Then in 1960 the Queen's Gallery was opened at Buckingham Palace, enabling the public to see a sequence of exhibitions of works from the Royal Collection; from time to time paintings may disappear from the walls of Hampton Court in order to be seen temporarily in this new context.

In recent years the Bronzino *Lady in Green* has been cleaned, also the head of a young man painted on panel and previously labelled School of Urbino. Research carried out at this time revealed that this work is not just an unknown youth painted by an unknown Italian artist, but a self-portrait by Raphael, and in beautiful condition.

All the most valuable paintings at Hampton Court are about to have a new home, but still in the Palace. A Renaissance Picture

Gallery is being planned; it will be situated in part of Wolsey's building, a range of smallish rooms overlooking Base Court from the south. Air-conditioning is being installed, the paintings are being made ready (the Bruegel for instance is being cleaned), and it is hoped that some of the Royal Collection now on loan – such as the Gentile da Fabriano altarpiece and the Mabuse *Adam and Eve* at the National Gallery will be displayed there alongside the best of the paintings normally on view in the Palace. So these fine things may at last be seen in a setting which is safe, appropriate and altogether delightful. The old Palace will have gained a new dimension.

SELECT BIBLIOGRAPHY

The principal source book for Hampton Court's history is Ernest Law's *History of Hampton Court Palace*, published by George Bell & Sons in three volumes, 1885, 1888 & 1891. Other books consulted were:

Adair, John *The Royal Palaces of Britain* Thames & Hudson, 1981

Aitken, James (ed.) *English Diaries of the XVI, XVII and XVIII Centuries* Penguin, 1941

Akrigg, G. P. V. *Jacobean Pageant* Hamish Hamilton, 1962

Brooke, John *King George II* Constable, 1972

Carleton, Dudley *Dudley Carleton to John Chamberlain, 1603–1624: Jacobean Letters,* ed. Maurice Lee, Jr., Rutger's University Press, New Jersey, 1972

Cavendish, George *The Life of Cardinal Wolsey* Oxford University Press, 1959

Chapman, Hester W. *The Last Tudor King* Jonathan Cape, 1958

Clarke, John *George III* Weidenfeld & Nicolson, 1972

Colvin, Howard *Royal Buildings* (R.I.B.A. Drawings Series) Country Life, 1968

Coward, Barry *The Stuart Age* Longman, 1980

Curtis, Gila *Queen Anne* Weidenfeld & Nicolson, 1973

Ede, Mary *Arts and Society in England under William and Mary* Stainer & Bell, 1979

Falkus, Christopher (ed.) *Private Lives of the Tudor Monarchs* Folio Society, 1974

Gaunt, William *Court Painting in England* Constable, 1980

Hackett, Francis *Henry the Eighth* Horace Liveright, N.Y., 1929

Hamilton, Elizabeth *The Illustrious Lady* Hamish Hamilton, 1980

Jourdain, Margaret *Stuart Furniture at Knole* Country Life, 1952

King, Ronald *The Quest for Paradise: a History of the World's Gardens* Whittet Windward, 1979

Luke, Mary M. *Catherine the Queen* Muller, 1968

Marillier, H. C. *The Tapestries at Hampton Court Palace* H.M.S.O., 1962

Marlow, Joyce *George I* Weidenfeld & Nicolson, 1973

Martindale, Andrew *The Triumph of Caesar* Oxford University Press, 1982

Millar, Sir Oliver *The Queen's Pictures* Weidenfeld & Nicolson, 1977

Millar, Sir Oliver *Pictures in the Royal Collection; Tudor, Stuart and Early Georgian Pictures* Phaidon, 1963

Millar, Sir Oliver *The Age of Charles I* (exhibition catalogue) The Tate Gallery, 1972

Millward, J. S. (ed.) *Portraits and Documents: Sixteenth Century* Hutchinson, 1961

Palmer, M. D. *Henry VIII* Longman, 1971

Plumb, J. H. and Wheldon, Sir Huw *Royal Heritage* B.B.C., 1977

Pollard, A. F. *Henry VII* Longman, 1971

Pollard, A. F. *Wolsey* Longman, 1951

Queen's Gallery, The *Holbein and the Court of Henry VIII* (exhibition catalogue), 1979

Queen's Gallery, The *Kings and Queens* (exhibition catalogue), 1982–83

Strong, Roy & Murrell, V. J. *Artists of the Tudor Court* (catalogue) V. & A. 1983

Trench, Charles Chenevix *George II* Allen Lane, 1973

Van der Zee, Henri and Barbara *William and Mary* Macmillan, 1973

Whinney, Margaret, *Wren* Thames & Hudson, 1971

Williams, Neville *Henry VIII and his Court* Weidenfeld & Nicolson, 1971

Winter, Carl *Elizabethan Miniatures* Penguin, 1943

Guidebooks, Booklets, Pamphlets etc.

Hampton Court Palace: Official Handbook by the late G. H. Chettle, John Charlton & Juliet Allan. H.M.S.O. 1982

Hampton Court Palace: Guide (6th Edition) G. H. Chettle & John Charlton. H.M.S.O. 1975

Hampton Court Palace: Guide G. H. Chettle. H.M.S.O. 1950, 1954

Historical Guide to the Royal Palace and Gardens at Hampton Court, with a new Historical Catalogue of the Pictures Ernest Law. George Bell & Sons, 1899

Hampton Court: a Collection of Documents compiled by Gerald Guinness. Jackdaw Publications, 1969

Photographs of Hampton Court Palace Royal Commission on Historical Monuments, 1938

Excavations at Hampton Court Palace D. Batchelor. Post-Medieval Archaeology, Vol. II, 1977

The Chapel Royal at Hampton Court G. D. Heath. Borough of Twickenham Local History Society, 1979

King William III Banqueting House, Hampton Court Palace Peter Curnow. H.M.S.O., 1958

The Royal Tennis Court at Hampton Court Palace booklet published by the Committee of the Royal Tennis Court, Hampton Court Palace

---

I have also been assisted by the following papers produced by my colleagues which, as far as I know, have not been published:

A Proposition regarding the Moat at Hampton Court Palace Gerald Heath & Gwyneth Williams

Entries relating to the King's Beasts in Henry VIII's Building Accounts for Hampton Court Palace Gerald Heath

The King's Great Staircase Gerald Heath & Philip Shearman

The Paradise Room Gerald Heath

The Maiano Medallions Gerald Heath & Gwyneth Williams

The Great Clock Gerald Heath

The Public Dining Room Gerald Heath

The Conversion of the Great Hall into a Theatre Gerald Heath

Index

Bold page numbers refer to illustrations. Entries in *italics* refer to poems, ballads and titles of some of the many paintings discussed in the text.